FOUNDATIONS OF MOD. . ..JIORY

General Editor: A. Goodwin

Emeritus Professor of Modern History, University of Manchester

Arms, Autarky and Aggression

A Study in German Foreign Policy, 1933–1939

by

WILLIAM CARR

Reader in Modern History, University of Sheffield

W·W·NORTON & COMPANY · INC·

NEW YORK

General Preface

In this study of the evolution of German foreign policy from 1933 to 1939, Dr Carr offers us a scholarly and revealing analysis of the internal conflicts provoked by Hitler's fanatical determination to enforce an unprecedented peacetime expansion of the German armed forces and to achieve the autarkic self-sufficiency of the German economy in terms of strategic war materials and food supplies. These objectives were clearly envisaged as the indispensable means to the pursuit of an inflexible and aggressive foreign policy, based on Hitler's own racialist ideologies, his long-term plans for Nazi domination of Eastern Europe and his obsessive resolve to achieve his ends at all costs.

English readers are already familiar with the repercussions of this policy on the international diplomacy of the period from the re-occupation of the Rhineland to the outbreak of the Second World War. It seems certain, however, that greater understanding of, and insight into, its tragic consequences, will result from those more recent revelations of the opposition to Hitler's foreign policy within the Third Reich which are here indicated rather than emphasized. In the longer perspective of history it is the reasons for the failure of this internal opposition, as well as the ineffectiveness and bankruptcy of Western 'appeasement' which will provide a more satisfactory explanation of the origins of the Second World War.

Despite the scepticism of some earlier critics, Dr Carr rightly contends that Hitler was a committed practitioner of the crude and pseudo-scientific theories of Social Darwinism, Geopolitics, and anti-semitism which he had absorbed in Vienna and Munich and he also shows how these ideologies affected the dictator's general attitude to the concrete issues of foreign policy after his seizure of power. The successive stages of Hitler's foreign policy are then outlined against the domestic background of

German rearmament and the largely unsuccessful efforts, after 1936, to create an autarkic framework for the German peacetime and war economy. The opposition which Hitler encountered at various times, and even as late as 1938, from the German Foreign Office, from the German High Command and from the more orthodox exponents of quasi-liberal economics, such as Schacht, is shown to have been frustrated by the Fuhrer's own demonic will-power, his unparalleled skill as a political tactician and by the apparent success of the Austrian *Anschluss*, the seizure of Czecho-slovakia and the conquest of Poland. Each of these international crises is studied in the light of the latest available evidence and Dr Carr's book is, in itself, a lucid and helpful guide to the present state of historical scholarship on the contentious issues raised by the outbreak of the Second World War.

A. GOODWIN

Contents

Abbreviations

DBFP	*Documents on British Foreign Policy, 1919–1939*
DDF	*Documents diplomatiques français, 1932–1939*
DGFP	*Documents on German Foreign Policy, 1918–1945*
Econ. H. R.	*Economic History Review*
HZ	*Historische Zeitschrift*
IMT	*Trial of the Major War Criminals before the International Military Tribunal*
JCH	*Journal of Contemporary History*
NCA	*Nazi Conspiracy and Aggression*
VFZ	*Vierteljahrshefte für Zeitgeschichte*

CHAPTER ONE

The Ideological Background

The primacy of foreign policy in which Hitler was a passionate believer was taken for granted in Imperial Germany. Since the days of Ranke geography, philosophy and history had been pressed into service to justify the belief that the conduct of foreign affairs was the supreme art of the statesman and an activity which must take precedence over all other aspects of policy. It was argued that a great nation with vulnerable frontiers and jealous neighbours was morally obliged to pursue an active foreign policy even at the expense of freedom at home. In a land where citizens were wont to exalt the state over civil society and to exaggerate the role of power factors in politics it was readily assumed that relations with other states were of supreme importance in the life of the nation. History pointed in the same direction. The rise of Prussia to greatness and the unification of Germany owed everything – so it seemed to contemporaries – to the might of Prussian arms and the skilful diplomacy of her kings and statesmen. The apparent success of Bismarck's complex diplomatic manœuvring after 1871 afforded further proof of the continuing importance of foreign policy for the survival of the new Reich.

German historical writing faithfully mirrored the prevailing ethos of the age. Most historians, completely dazzled by Bismarck's achievements, believed that *Staatsgeschichte* was the only subject worthy of a serious historian's pen. Economic and social history was looked down upon as a mundane study of secondary importance fit only for obscure local historians. 'National' historians positively resented the notion that foreign policy might be more fruitfully studied in its socio-economic context rather than in complete isolation. Only when the Reich of 1871 had disappeared for ever at the end of the Second World War, did *Staatsgeschichte* cease to dominate historical writing. Today a new generation of West German historians, untouched by the atavistic nationalism of Wilhelminian Germany, reject the basic assumptions underlying the work of the great historians of Imperial Germany such as Sybel, Mommsen, Treitschke and Lenz. Indeed the wheel has come almost full circle. These young historians speak not of the primacy of foreign policy but of the primacy of internal policy, for it is their contention that domestic affairs shaped imperial foreign policy, not *vice versa*, as the older generation of historians maintained.

All this is a very recent development. In 1918 there was no trace of a change of outlook among German historians. On the contrary, defeat gave a new lease of life to orthodox thinking. Popular resentment against the Versailles '*Diktat*' and widespread hatred of the arch-enemy France obliged successive Weimar governments to accord a very high priority to foreign policy with notable success in the late 1920s. As the shadows fell across the republic in the early 1930s, Chancellor Bruening reaffirmed the supreme importance of foreign policy. In the midst of severe economic dislocation and growing political extremism he pinned his hopes for the survival of constitutional government to external success over reparations and disarmament.

Paradoxically enough it was Hitler, the avowed enemy of parliamentary democracy, who promised to reverse this order of priorities when the Nazis came to power. 'In contrast to our own official government,' he told West German industrialists in January 1932, 'I cannot see any hope for the resurrection of Germany if we regard the foreign policies of Germany as the primary factor: the primary necessity is the restoration of a sound national body-politic armed to strike.'[1]

In fact that remark did not signify the end of the primacy of foreign policy. Earlier in his address Hitler argued that the people must eventually 'turn its energies outwards' in order to survive. The point he wished to drive home, in order to win the support of powerful industrialists, was that the Nazis would destroy parliamentary democracy and mobilise the will of the nation before embarking upon an energetic foreign policy. Muted though the message was for tactical reasons, Hitler did not disguise his belief that a forward foreign policy was still the primary objective of the Nazi movement. For Hitler 'the primacy of internal policy' was a temporary phenomenon only, a tactical necessity until such time as foreign policy could resume its traditional primacy.

[1] N. Baynes, *Hitler's Speeches, 1922–1939* (Oxford, 1942) I, p. 828.

From the earliest days of his association with the Nazi party Hitler displayed a passionate interest in foreign affairs. His general views on the subject are expounded at length in two works dating from this period: *Mein Kampf* and *Hitler's Secret Book* (*Zweites Buch*). *Mein Kampf*, which became the bible of the Nazi movement and netted a fortune for the author, was dictated in Landsberg prison after the abortive *Putsch* of 1923 and completed in 1925. The *Secret Book*, written in 1928, was not published in Hitler's lifetime possibly because as Nazi fortunes improved, Hitler chose to cultivate a more moderate tone on foreign affairs. *Mein Kampf*, it must be remembered, was no casual exercise to while away monotony. It was written to establish the author as the dominant theorist as well as the leading orator in the party, and is therefore a major source for the study of Hitler. The same applies to the *Secret Book* in which he re-stated in greater detail and more forcibly what he had said about foreign affairs in *Mein Kampf*. Written five years after the latter, the *Secret Book* represents the final stage in the clarification of Hitler's ideas since his early beginnings as a nationalist agitator in 1919.

To what extent did Hitler reveal his true intentions in these works? Over the years opinions have been sharply divided. A leading authority once described *Mein Kampf* as a 'blueprint for aggression'.[2] Only in a very general sense is that true. If by blueprint we mean a detailed timetable for aggression that cannot be found in *Mein Kampf* or anywhere else. Nor could a precise blueprint have ever existed. The history of the 1930s shows quite clearly that Hitler was as much at the mercy of events as other statesmen. Like them he had to alter course from time to time for tactical reasons. The main difference was that he exploited opportunities with a consummate skill and tenacity of purpose which they conspicuously lacked. Tactical considerations governed his attitude to other aspects of Nazi policy as well. For example, in the early days radical elements were strong in the party and left their mark on the party programme. Safely in power, Hitler jettisoned without scruple the whole of their lower middle-class 'socialism'. Even in *Mein Kampf* he did not disguise his complete cynicism about detailed programmes; they were a means to the end of power and expendable once the end was attained.

[2] H. Trevor-Roper, 'A. J. P. Taylor, Hitler and the war', *Encounter*, July 1961, p. 90.

Evidence of a high degree of opportunism in Hitler has led some historians, notably Alan Taylor, to conclude that he was basically an empty-headed power seeker and opportunist whose ruminations in *Mein Kampf* and in the *Secret Book* had little bearing on his subsequent conduct.[3] That might well have been the case with the average career politician grooming himself for high office and only too anxious to live down youthful literary indiscretions. Apart from the documentary evidence, to be examined presently, a consideration of Hitler's personality raises serious doubts about the validity of this interpretation.

François-Poncet, the perceptive representative of France in Berlin from 1931 to 1938, once wrote that Hitler was no normal human being but 'a character out of the pages of Dostoevsky, a man possessed'.[4] By any reckoning Hitler's political gifts were outstanding. Unquestionably the greatest demagogue of the century, an orator of immense power, virtually unrivalled in his uncanny understanding of the mass media of communications, he was also an organizer of great ability and a politician of remarkable acumen able to hold the party together with superb skill through periods of stress and strain. It is equally evident that he was an abnormal personality though psychiatrists will continue to differ in their diagnoses. Contemporaries are agreed that Hitler was a moody, restless and explosive character, lacking in human affection for the most part, inordinately suspicious of mankind in general, domineering, opinionated – positively paranoid in some of his views – and above all a man of extraordinary willpower who displayed fantastic singleness of purpose in his search for supreme power. What drove him on was not ordinary human ambition but a fanatical belief that his destiny was indissolubly linked with Germany's.

His outlook changed hardly at all with the passage of the years. At the very end, living a shadowy troglodyte existence in the chancellery bunker pounded by Russian shells, Hitler was still the street orator of a quarter of a century before. To the very end he nursed the same violent prejudices and bitter animosities, burst into the same towering rages when he encountered opposition, displayed the same irrational confidence in his own infallibility –

[3] A. J. P. Taylor, *The Origins of the Second World War* (London, 1961), pp. 69, 108, 134, 204.
[4] A. François-Poncet, *The fateful years* (London, 1949), p. 292.

and still exerted a strange fascination over many of his close associates. It has been suggested, though the medical evidence is admittedly inconclusive, that he suffered from Parkinson's disease; if so, this might help to explain his extraordinary mental rigidity and utter disregard for opposing viewpoints towards the end of his life. All in all, it does not seem unreasonable to assume that the thoughts this strange man committed to paper in Landsberg prison at the age of thirty-six probably represented sincerely-held beliefs from which he did not deviate for the next twenty-five years.

The documentary evidence points strongly in the same direction. Generally speaking, Hitler disliked putting pen to paper. There are no bulging files of Führer correspondence; Hitler left no memoirs (apart from the *Table Talk*); he kept no diary; he wrote few letters and made no marginal comments on official documents. The dull time-consuming routine of the office desk was alien to his restless and somewhat indolent Bohemian spirit. He much preferred to discuss problems unofficially with intimate associates at the Berghof, his retreat on the Hoher Goll, a mountain south of Berchtesgaden, where he spent most weekends before 1939. This irregular way of life has grave disadvantages for historians. It makes it extraordinarily difficult, if not impossible, to trace the evolution of his policies with exactitude. Nevertheless, the few records we possess of Hitler's confidential addresses in the 1930s to members of his entourage, high-ranking party officials and army commanders reveal a surprising degree of consistency in respect of the objectives of Nazi foreign policy.

Of course, the fact that Hitler made frequent references to a few general concepts is not in itself proof positive that these ideas exerted decisive influence on day-to-day policy. Andreas Hillgruber warns against such oversimplification in a brilliant study of the years 1940–41 which shows that the relationship between Hitler's basic thought patterns and unpredictable temperament on the one hand, and the tactical necessities and shifting balance of power on the other is immensely complex and defies precise analysis.[5] Attempts to clarify the relationship have to take account of yet another factor, namely that Hitler was a skilful manipulator of men and situations, a *Realpolitiker* of outstanding ability who

[5] *Hitlers Strategie. Politik und Kriegsführung, 1940–1941* (Frankfurt a.M., 1965).

showed great perception and cunning in the choice of arguments most likely to impress his immediate audience. It is unwise to accept what Hitler said on any occasion as a precise indication of his immediate intentions. He often spoke for effect as those close to him were well aware. For that reason they were least impressed by his long, rambling and repetitive monologues. Significantly enough, he was displeased if followers took him too literally. The 'irrevocable' decisions of which the Führer was inordinately fond were not necessarily his last word but rather an emphatic assertion of what he happened to believe or wanted his audience to believe at a particular moment in time.

It is important to remind ourselves that Hitler's foreign policy cannot be studied in a vacuum totally divorced from life in Nazi Germany. Without the central figure of Hitler Nazi success in 1933 would have been inconceivable; one has only to look at film records of the period to appreciate the immense influence this man exerted over the mass of the people during and after the rise to power. East German historians, blinkered by an inflexible Marxism, grossly underestimate the element of personal charisma and insist on depicting Hitler as a shadowy figure, the helpless puppet of monopoly capitalism. It is easy to see that this militates against a proper understanding of the past. However, non-Marxists should temper their strictures with the reflection that it is fatally easy to fall into the opposite pitfall and exaggerate the role of the individual in history. To suppose that one man by sheer force of personality alone forced his views on the mass of the people would betray an equal lack of historical insight. The truth is that Hitler was the product of a particular socio-economic situation. Overwhelmed by an economic disaster which shook the capitalist system to its foundations, large numbers of Germans turned to Hitler as to a saviour. These circumstances alone made it possible for him to play on the disillusionment of the masses with the old order and exploit their hopes for a better future. Out of this situation arose an intimate relationship between leader and followers which endured until well into the war. Whatever permanency the regime possessed depended very largely on the maintenance of this delicate relationship as Hitler was well aware.

The need to win and retain mass support during the rise to power in the early 1930s exerted some influence on the kind of foreign policy Hitler advocated in public. The resentment and frustration of the masses had to be directed against easily identifiable foes in order to keep disparate elements marching in step. Attacks on the Versailles Treaty, outward symbol of German 'humiliation', coupled with appeals for a great national awakening and the union of all German-speaking people never failed to arouse enthusiasm in audiences accustomed to the idea that Germany had been shabbily treated in 1919. Violent onslaughts on democracy, Marxism and Jewry, 'the unholy trinity' blamed by Hitler for the present discontents, evoked a similar response from disillusioned voters eager for scapegoats. But whereas Hitler in the 1920s spoke frequently of the need to acquire living space in the east, in the 1930s there were fewer references to eastward expansion because a party with power in its grasp could not afford to scare away potential supporters by alarmist talk of aggression.

That does not mean that the quest for living space was of no account in Hitler's calculations after 1933. On the contrary, eastward expansion remained the ultimate rationale of Hitler's whole policy as will be shown later. Tactically, it was an invaluable rallying cry to spur the Nazi movement onward when spirits flagged and to keep alive the belief of rank-and-file Nazis in Germany's glorious future. Vague and open-ended the concept most certainly was, and capable of various interpretations. For all that living space symbolized the imperialist content of Nazi foreign policy and remained the ultimate goal of a regime which gloried in action for its own sake and for that reason could not rest on its laurels for long.

Fritz Fischer's seminal work, *Griff nach der Weltmacht*,* has done more than any other work to transform the attitude of West German historians to the origins of the First World War. One of the controversies reanimated by this book is the old argument about the continuity of German foreign policy from William II to Hitler. Historians have had to reconsider confident assertions that Nazi foreign policy differed fundamentally from that of previous regimes. That there are important elements of continuity is obvious in as much as a country's foreign policy is determined in large measure by geographical, economic and socio-political factors. By drawing attention to the elements of continuity, the

Germany's Aims in the First World War (London and New York, 1967).

Fischer school has enormously enriched our understanding of the pre-1914 period. However, similarities between Hitler's policy and that of Imperial Germany should not be given undue weight. The real difference is surely qualitative. The schemes drawn up in wartime Germany for the domination of Eastern Europe pale into insignificance compared with the appalling ruthlessness of the Nazi extermination campaign in Russia between 1941 and 1944, a campaign conducted with the deliberate intention of transforming the area into a huge colonial dependency of the Reich where the eastern peoples would slave for ever for their Nazi masters. In this very real sense one can still maintain that Hitler's policy was uniquely different from that of preceding regimes.

Ruthlessness towards opponents, whether fellow-Germans or racial 'inferiors', was essentially an expression of the Nazi belief that Europe was on the eve of a cataclysmic upheaval certain to shake to pieces the old order with its outworn bourgeois values, a concept curiously akin to the Marxist belief in the imminent demise of the capitalist order. This revolutionary undertone runs like a red thread through Hitler's recorded utterances from the conversation with Breiting in 1931 to the *Table Talk* of 1941–2. The First World War had broken the spell of eternal peace, so the argument ran, and liberal democracy was hastening to the grave mortally wounded by the Depression. Here the parallel with Marxism ceased. For the future lay not with the proletariat of all lands but with the young vigorous nations, Germany and Italy. Nazi ambitions could not be realized without revolutionary change. Enduring greatness for Germany was impossible in the sedate setting of the old bourgeois-conservative order of aristocracy and middle class. The alliance of steel and rye, linch-pin of William II's Reich, had outlived its usefulness and would be swept away in the Third Reich. In its place would arise a National Socialist Order based not on divisive class privilege but on the unifying concept of race. It was the historic mission of the Nazi movement to give birth to a new racially pure ruling élite recruited regardless of class or creed to lord it over subject peoples in a Greater German Reich. Herein lay Hitler's real claim to fame. In power he took absolutely seriously the crude and vulgarized notion, picked up twenty years before in the street cafés of Vienna and Munich, that biology mattered more in the life of a great nation than cultural achievements or economic power. What the class struggle was to Marxism, the racial struggle was to National Socialism, the inner law of history and the central axis around which the theory and practice of the Third Reich revolved.

Hitler's foreign policy is only properly intelligible as an expression of his racialist philosophy. Most people think of him as a nationalist agitator. That seems reasonable enough for did he not make his reputation by denouncing the Versailles Treaty for separating millions of Germans from the fatherland in defiance of the principle of self-determination and by calling stridently for the union of all German-speaking people in one Reich? *Ein Volk, ein Reich, ein Führer* was the Nazi slogan best known outside Germany. In fact, old-fashioned nationalism of this variety was intended primarily for mass consumption. It was a means to an end, not the end itself. In private Hitler made no secret of his belief that the day of the nation state was over and about to be superseded by a new age of imperialism. The struggle for living space, not the improvement of existing political frontiers, would determine the nature of foreign policy in this new age. Seen in this wider perspective, the incorporation of German minorities in the German fatherland assumes subsidiary importance. The recovery of German Austria and the Sudetenland were only steps on the road to the real goal which was to make Germany the dominant power in Europe at the expense of racially 'inferior' peoples in the east. This ambition clearly could not be realised within the frontiers of Imperial, much less Weimar Germany. Perfectly logically, Hitler was not remotely interested in the recovery of the 1914 frontiers. In the *Secret Book* he poured contempt on bourgeois politicians who demanded these frontiers. No greater sin against one's own people was imaginable than to go to war merely to extend the frontier from Herbesthal to Lüttich. For those intrepid readers who ventured beyond the first few pages of *Mein Kampf* – and tragically too few bothered to do so or believed what they read if they did so – the truth was stated bluntly and uncompromisingly: 'We National Socialists consequently draw a line beneath the foreign policy tendency of our pre-war period. We take up where we broke off six hundred years ago. We stop the endless German movement to the south and west, and turn our gaze toward the land in the east. At long last we break off the colonial and commercial policy of the pre-war period and shift to the soil policy of the future.'[6] The new policy had even graver implications. If the conquest of land in the east resulted only in the enslavement of Slav peoples, the new *Reich* would not survive. Blood, not language, counted. Germanized Czechs and Poles were no asset to Germany. The only way of making German domination permanent was to oust the native population and settle German farmers on the rich soil of the Ukraine. So from the mid-1920s Hitler was committed by his racialism to an aggressive and ruthless policy far exceeding the dreams of the German upper classes during the First World War. Nor did he trouble to disguise the fact that these plans meant war with Russia. 'If we speak of soil in Europe today', he wrote with appalling candour in *Mein Kampf*, 'we can primarily have in mind only Russia and her vassal border states.'[7]

It was suggested earlier that it is a mistake to think of Hitler as a ruthless power seeker without a specific ideology of his own but with an infinite capacity for exploiting other peoples' ideas. Until comparatively recently the latter view, popularized by a renegade Nazi, Hermann Rauschning, was generally accepted by historians. Hugh Trevor-Roper was one of the first to challenge this interpretation and point out that Hitler was undeniably a man of ideas, however crude and repellent they appear to civilised men.[8] Recent research has confirmed the correctness of this analysis. No one would claim that Hitler was an original thinker. A senior civil servant close to him likened Hitler to a reflector which intercepts light rays and transmits them onward in an intensified form.[9] Hitler prided himself on being a rational man of science but like many self-educated people he fell easy prey to pseudo-scientific theories circulating in the coffee houses of Vienna and Munich before 1914. From newspapers and popular tracts he imbibed the essentials of the racialism and anti-semitism which were his stock-in-trade for the rest of his life. It may be useful at this point to explain how these theories moulded his attitude to foreign affairs.

[6] *Mein Kampf*, trans. R. Manheim (Boston, 1943), p. 654.
[7] *Mein Kampf*, p. 654.
[8] Cf. preface to *The Table Talk of Adolf Hitler, 1941–4* (London, 1953).
[9] O. Meissner, *Staatssekretär unter Ebert-Hindenburg-Hitler* (Mannheim, 1950), p. 617.

A crude and unsophisticated Social Darwinism allied to a belief in the innate superiority of the Aryan race formed the corner-stones of Hitler's political philosophy. From first to last he believed that life was a hard and bitter struggle for existence, a purely biological process and nothing more. Men were no different in kind from beasts of the field. Therefore, hunger and love, 'the regents of life', were the determinants of man's conduct. To maintain themselves men had to satisfy their hunger, and by satisfying their desire for love man perpetuated the species. But, as the space at mens' disposal was limited by the physical confines of the globe, struggle between races was the inevitable consequence of mens' attempts to satisfy their desires. In this struggle for survival compassion for the weak, the sick and the old and concern for moral values was 'unscientific'. To Hitler the superstructure of human rights, painfully constructed over the centuries, counted for nothing compared with the basic urge to maintain and propagate the Aryan race and the German people in particular. This could be achieved only by territorial expansion at the expense of weaker peoples exactly as the strong preyed on the weak in the natural order. 'In struggle I see the destiny of all human beings', he declared, 'no one can escape the struggle if he does not want to be defeated.'[10] History was reduced to an account of man's relentless struggle for survival and for living space. Politics was simply the art of conducting this struggle; internal policy the art of ensuring that a people had the power and resolution to wage the struggle; and foreign policy the art of establishing 'a sound and viable relationship between a nation's population and growth on the one hand and the quantity and quality of its soil on the other.'[11]

After the war another pseudo-science, geopolitics, exerted some influence on Hitler. Karl Haushofer, a much-travelled Bavarian general, popularized the geographical theories of Kjellen, Ratzel and Mackinder at Munich University in the 1920s. Among his disciples was an intense young man called Rudolf Hess, a former officer and close associate of Hitler's. Through his enthusiastic pupil Haushofer was introduced to Hitler in 1922 and probably visited him in Landsberg prison. Haushofer kept Hitler supplied with books including Ratzel's

[10] *IMT*, XXVI, p. 329.
[11] *Mein Kampf*, p. 643; cf. *Hitler's Secret Book* (New York, 1961), p. 24.

Politische Geographie, a seminal work which interpreted geographical data in terms of evolution and natural selection. The
eastward expansion advocated so zealously by chauvinist-
minded geopoliticians at the Munich Institute was, of course, a
well-established theme in German history. In Hitler's youth the
Pan Germans were the most vociferous and fanatical advocates
of eastward expansion. What influence Pan Germanism exerted
on Hitler is uncertain but very likely he was acquainted with their
crude literature. Nor, when considering Hitler's attitude to
expansion, should one forget that he was Austrian by birth. From
1909 to 1913 he lived at the heart of the multi-national Habsburg
Empire, an experience which left an indelible stamp on his
opinions. The embryonic racialism and anti-semitism of school
days in Linz was deepened in Vienna where he learnt to hate
Marxism and parliamentary government and to despise the Habs-
burgs for their 'criminal failure' to stem the rising tide of Slav
nationalism. From this period stems his profound contempt for
Slav peoples in general and for Czechs in particular – the
influence of Schönerer's Pan Germanism was probably decisive
here. The grandiose schemes of the geopoliticians for the sub-
jugation of Slav peoples supplied Hitler with a bogus 'scientific'
explanation for ingrained racial prejudices and probably helped
him decide – as he had done by 1924 – that Germany's destiny
lay in the east.[12] From the geopoliticians he learnt to appreciate
the strategic advantages of expansion, i.e. the belief that in the
air age the military defence of states would increasingly depend
on their physical extent. Or, as he put it in a speech in the 1920s:
'With the aeroplane our German territory is crossed in barely
four hours. It is no longer an area of innate protection such as
Russia whose geographical expanse is a power in itself, a safety
coefficient.'[13]

Finally, anti-semitism. Hitler quickly succumbed to the notion
that race, not religion, was the only 'scientific' basis for opposition

[12] Before 1924 Hitler does not appear to have dissented from the general Nazi
view that Russia, freed from 'Jewish bolshevism', would be an ideal ally for
Germany against France. After 1924 nothing is heard of this argument until
1939. Prior to 1924 Nazi propaganda contains few references to the 'inferiority',
of Slav peoples. Cf. W. Horn, 'Ein unbekannter Aufsatz aus dem Frühjahr
1924' in *VFZ*, 16, 1968.
[13] H. Preis (ed.), *Adolf Hitler in Franken. Reden aus der Kampfzeit* (Nuremberg,
1939), p. 79; cf. *Hitler's Secret Book*, pp. 73–4, 125–7.

to Jewry. Anti-semitism, as expounded by Lanz von Liebenfels in the newssheet *Ostara* in Hitler's Vienna days, unlocked several doors. No doubt as the party grew in the late 1920s Hitler, the supreme political realist, appreciated that Jews were convenient scapegoats who could be blamed for all the ills besetting Germany. If that had been all there was to it, Hitler in power would soon have abandoned the visceral politics of the gutter. Unfortunately for mankind the roots of Hitler's anti-semitism extended far deeper than the cynical calculations of the party boss. Hitler lived in a nightmare world of his own making where sinister Jewish wire-pullers lurked behind every movement of which he disapproved from Freemasonry to Marxism. Although his hatred of Jews was deeply irrational, clearly paranoid and possibly pathological in intensity, behind it lay a fairly coherent doctrine, a rationalisation of the irrational which he elaborated in full in the *Secret Book*.

Hitler's starting point was an assumption that only higher races were capable of building states and that states were the essential basis for the independence of a people. The Jew, as a member of a lower race, was *ipso facto* incapable of productive activity. Still, the self-preservation instinct and the desire to propagate their own species were as deeply rooted in Jews as in other peoples, and to achieve these ends a state was essential. Therefore, in the interests of survival, the Jew 'insinuated' his way into higher races where he lived a parasitic existence by fraud, deception and cunning, battening on the toil of honest men – Hitler maintained that only higher races had a proper social concept of work. The Jews' ultimate ambition was to deflect the higher races from their God-given mission of expansion, the most important activity, be it noted, in the life of a people. How would the Jews do this? By spreading the pernicious doctrines of internationalism, pacifism and democracy. Internationalism was the most deadly poison imaginable. It 'denationalized' peoples, anaesthetized them and stifled their natural desire to expand at the expense of weaker peoples. Pacifism was hardly less pernicious for it destroyed the martial virtues required for expansion. Lastly, democracy which by equating inferior races with higher races inverted the law of nature whereby the latter had dominion over the former. Throughout recorded history the Jews had sought to attain their ends by burrowing underground in every state. From the Exodus out of Egypt to the French and Russian Revolutions the Jews were responsible for every revolutionary uprising. Once Jewish revolutionaries seized power, as in Russia, they promptly liquidated the old ruling class in order to strengthen their hold over the leaderless masses. Like other anti-semites, Hitler believed in a vast world conspiracy co-ordinating the subversive activities of Jews in all lands. Chameleon-like, the Jew adopted protective colouration wherever he went; sometimes the liberal pacifist, sometimes the plutocratic capitalist exploiter, sometimes the Marxist agitator; the roles were interchangeable but the goal of world domination described in the *Protocols of Zion* remained as unchanging as the stars. Bolshevism was the latest and most serious instrument of the Jewish world conspirators and against it all efforts must be directed. For should the Jews succeed in establishing their tyranny over the earth and prevent the strong peoples expanding, this would lead inevitably to the depopulation of the earth, 'the funeral wreath of mankind' in Hitler's dramatic phrase. Paradoxically, that would be the end of Jewry because being parasites the Jews would perish when their victims died. Emboldened by their victory in Russia, the Jews were redoubling their efforts in Germany defiling the purity of the Aryan race and corrupting the national virility of the people while international Jewish capital held the country in thrall under the Versailles shackles. Hitler saw it as his mission to frustrate the plans of international Jewry by waging ruthless and remorseless warfare on Jews inside and outside Germany. Internal and external policy were inextricably intertwined at the very heart of Hitler's *Weltanschauung*, each impacting on the other and both reflecting Hitler's fanatical obsession with racial purity.

An aggressive foreign policy was already implicit in the pseudo-Darwinian theory that virile peoples had an inalienable right to expand at the cost of weaker peoples. What anti-semitism did was to remove any lingering doubt about the advisability of eastward expansion. The hard fact was that adequate living space could only be obtained at the expense of Russia, theoretically a potential ally against France. If in addition Germany had a duty to combat 'Jewish bolshevism' before it engulfed Germany, then eastward expansion was mandatory for National Socialists. Self-interest and ideological prejudice happily coincided, a stroke of great good fortune for the Nazis as Hitler readily admitted. Of the difficulty of the task he was setting Germany, Hitler had no ink-ling. In *Mein Kampf* he maintained that Russia was 'ripe for collapse' because Jews were not state builders but only 'a ferment of decomposition'. It is true that he made much of the 'Russian peril' in the 1930s. That was simply for tactical reasons, not because he had any appreciation of the fact that the Five Year Plan was laying the basis of a mighty industrial and military complex.[14] In fairness, it must be admitted that events such as the purges of 1937 misled many experienced observers into supposing that Russia was a power of no account.

Both in *Mein Kampf* and in the *Secret Book* Hitler insisted that the mainspring of foreign policy was not economic self-interest, as Marxists argued, but simply and solely the solemn duty to preserve the racial group. Economics were relegated to a quite subordinate place in Hitler's scheme of things; 'the sword has to stand before the plough and an army before economics', so he wrote.[15] He never wearied of assuring close associates that economic problems could always be solved by willpower what-ever so-called 'experts' pretended. Not surprisingly, there is relatively little in *Mein Kampf* or in the *Secret Book* about econ-omics, and what Hitler has to say on the subject is garbled and deeply coloured by folkish and anti-semitic prejudices. Yet it would be wrong to suppose that Hitler was uninterested in economics as has been suggested.[16] Though completely without formal training in economics, he had, if not a coherent theory of economics, then at least 'a substitute for an economic theory' which was closely allied to his view of foreign policy. The essentials of his politico-economic ideas are contained in those sections of both works where he discusses what he considered, in his rather primitive fashion, to be the basic problem of feeding Germany's growing population.

At first sight Hitler's 'blood and soil' policy seems indistinguish-able from the classic imperialist answer to the problem of growing

---

[14] Occasionally his utterances had a prophetic ring about them; in 1931 he remarked that Germany must complete her plans 'before the Soviet Union becomes a world power and before the 7 million square miles of territory held by the USA becomes the arsenal of World Jewry. These colossal powers are still asleep. When they wake up it is the end for Germany.' E. Calic, *Ohne Maske. Hitler-Breiting Geheimgespräche* (Frankfurt, 1969), pp. 71–2.

[15] *Hitler's Secret Book*, p. 99.

[16] A. Bullock, *Hitler: A study in tyranny* (London, 1962), pp. 152, 402.

numbers pressing on limited resources.[17] In fact, the expansion of
the German population was as much an objective of this policy
as the reason for it. As the Nazis saw it, population and land were
to spur each other on endlessly with the preservation of the race
as the ultimate objective. If population exceeded resources
Germany would have to acquire new land to alleviate the pressure. Conversely, population must be encouraged to outstrip
resources in order to create the very dilemma from which expansion had just rescued Germany. Consequently birth control was
utterly abhorrent to Hitler, not so much because it reduced the
size of a people – though he alleged that it had denied life to more
people in one year than had been killed in all the wars from the
French Revolution onwards – but because contraception robbed
a nation of political leaders as these were usually not the first or
second born but came towards the end of large families.

Nor did Hitler believe that much could be done to grow more
food at home by intensive cultivation of the soil. Even if this were
possible, any increased yield would be swallowed up in rising
living standards. Later on he argued that intensive use of
artificial fertilizers would eventually exhaust Germany's soil.
Land redistribution, particularly the break-up of East Prussian
latifundia was not the answer either. But the real objection to
increased home production slipped out in *Mein Kampf* when Hitler
remarked that it was positively undesirable for the Germans to
believe for one moment that the food problem could be solved
within existing frontiers because people would then lose the will
to expand.

As Hitler saw it, Germany had to choose between a 'territorial'
policy and a 'commercial' policy. Hitherto Germany, like other
advanced industrial countries, had pursued a 'commercial'
policy, i.e. essential food and raw material imports were financed
by exporting capital goods. Hitler bitterly opposed international
trade not on economic, but on ideological grounds. Once the
spirit of commercialism gripped a nation, moral degeneration

[17] Population increased from 61 millions in 1914 to 67·8 millions in 1936.
Despite Goebbel's wild talk in 1939 of a population of 130 millions by 1989,
computations of the German Statistical Office suggested a figure of 80·5 millions
in 1970 gradually declining to 77 millions by 2000. The excess of births over
deaths 1934–7 was 478,000 compared with 773,000 in 1901–10. Hitler's overpopulation argument was, in fact, already outdated by the time he came to
power.

followed inevitably, a familiar lamentation in high conservative circles for over a century. Hitler spelt out the consequences for post-war Germany. Agriculture had declined greatly in status. 'Unbridled industrialism' disturbed the natural balance between town and country, spawning vast unhealthy cities peopled by resentful proletariats. Moral standards were eroded by internationalism. 'Art bolshevism' had poisoned Germany's cultural life. The economic sinews of the nation were in the hands of international Jewry operating behind the stock exchanges. And, most disastrous of all, pacifism and Marxism were rotting the fighting spirit of the nation. In short, 'commercialism' was paving the way for the decline of the German race and must be opposed at all costs.

Four years later in the *Secret Book* Hitler did attempt to advance economic arguments against 'commercialism'. He pointed out that in an increasingly industrialized world Germany was bound to face greater difficulties. The struggle for markets had been intensified by the rise of the USA as a major trading nation. Economic power, large internal markets and advanced techniques made the Americans formidable competitors, especially in the automobile industry. In the face of this competition German price cutting to cheapen exports stood little chance of success. Even so Hitler's objections to 'commercialism' were still basically ideological. Thus he attributed American success in the last resort not so much to their economic power and living space as to the high racial quality of their immigrants. If Germany was to resist the North American bid for world hegemony – which he thought she must do one day – then success would depend primarily on her ability to preserve the purity of her own racial stock.[18]

Hitler was equally critical of the effects 'commercialism' had on foreign policy. Imperial Germany's bid for the peaceful economic conquest of the world – a most dubious historical assumption to say the least – had been the height of folly. In the first place, a pacific policy was intrinsically wrong because it implied the abandonment of power politics and territorial expansion, both essential ingredients of a 'respectable' foreign policy. Secondly,

[18] In the early 1930s Hitler changed his mind about the USA. Seeking an explanation for her economic weakness, he concluded that she was, after all, a racial medley, 'a mongrel society', constituting no threat to Europe. Cf. G. Weinberg, 'Hitler's image of the United States', *AHR*, 69, 1964.

attempts to wage economic warfare against powerful nations such as Britain always ended in open warfare. That was the lesson of 1914. *Weltpolitik*, colonial rivalry and the navy combined to alienate Britain from Germany, and could do so again. By the time he dictated *Mein Kampf*, Hitler's attitude to Britain had undergone a complete transformation. In 1919 he bracketed Britain and France together as mortal enemies. At that time Italy and possibly Russia seemed the most likely allies for Germany in her struggle against Versailles. By 1924 sharp differences between Britain and France over the Ruhr occupation made him change his mind. France always remained the arch-enemy but in Britain he now saw a future ally. Whether this was a consequence or a cause of his change of front towards Russia is open to question. What is certain is that Hitler's political strategy had finally crystallized out into a coherent programme: in alliance with Britain and Italy a National Socialist Germany would eliminate France as a factor in European affairs, and then turned eastwards to sezie living space from Russia.

It seems more than likely that this programme constituted only the first stage in Germany's rise to greatness. Hitler was manifestly a continental politician whose ambition was to make Germany dominant in Europe '*so oder so*', to use one of his favourite phrases. Nevertheless, even in *Mein Kampf* he declared that Germany 'would either be a world power or there will be no Germany'.[19] This ambiguous remark was not elaborated upon either here or in the *Secret Book*, probably because the second stage of world domination lay in the distant future shrouded in obobscurity: to discuss it would only divert attention from the task in hand. Such slender evidence as we possess suggests that he envisaged a decisive struggle for world domination perhaps a century hence between Britain and Germany, though at times he spoke of war between the USA and a Europe united under Germany with Britain as a Germany ally. The outcome would be world domination, the logical end of his racial policy. It will be seen later that the problems of the second stage began to concern him on the eve of the Second World War and exerted a not inconsiderable influence on naval strategy.

In *Mein Kampf* Hitler painted a glowing picture of the advantages of a 'territorial' policy. Ideological considerations loomed

[19] *Mein Kampf*, p. 654.

large in the balance sheet. In the new *Reich* the farming community, sheet anchor of a healthy and racially-sound society, would be restored to a privileged position. Once the grip of Jewish bankers over the economy had been broken, the unhealthy domination of industry and commerce would cease. A proper balance would be struck between supply and demand so that 'the subsistence of the people as a whole (would become) more or less independent of foreign countries and thus help to secure the freedom of the state and the independence of the nation particularly in difficult periods.'[20]

This fanciful picture of a society purged of 'Jewish contamination' where industry and commerce would be relegated to a subordinate role in the interests of agrarian self-sufficiency was not just an aberration typical of eccentric folkish enthusiasts of the pre-war and post-war period. It reflected at a deeper level the longing of the broad mass of Hitler's followers for a haven of economic security in a storm-tossed world, a sentiment which lay at the very heart of the National Socialist philosophy. Liberal capitalism tied to world markets and dedicated to the unrestrained pursuit of wealth had little appeal for the Nazis. Like the *Handwerker* of the mid-nineteenth century, they were seeking an economic order where a 'point of equilibrium' could be attained to insulate the individual against the divisive effects of economic growth and rapid social change. Rural life appealed greatly to the Nazis on account of its conservative static quality and because it was supposed that the farming community possessed in pristine splendour those manly virtues of patriotism, heroism and self-sacrifice which the Nazis prized so highly.[21]

However, the Nazi attitude to growth had perforce to be somewhat ambivalent. Up to a point growth was essential for the achievement of other objectives. The creation of a strong Germany took precedence over everything else and for this purpose a strong army was essential. That in turn predicated a flourishing industrial base. Certainly special attention was paid to rural life in the Third Reich but not at the expense of industrial investment which increased steadily after 1933.

[20] *Mein Kampf*, p. 138.
[21] Cf. Hitler to the farmers assembled on the Bückeberg, 7 October 1933: 'You must be the class which does not provide merely the peoples' food; you must also supply the strength of will.' N. Baynes, *op. cit.*, I, p. 873.

The tension between the need for growth and the desire for stability was resolved to some extent by the commitment to living space. The longing of Hitler's followers for a secure and stable economic order coincided with his own predeliction for a self-sufficient economy. Not only was dependence on world markets incompatible with the freedom and independence Hitler demanded for Germany militarily and politically, but it left the people at the mercy of capricious economic forces. A closed economy sheltering the people from the vagaries of international finance seemed the only guarantee of economic stability. The practical difficulty was that Germany could not achieve self-sufficiency within existing frontiers. Her economic needs could be fully satisfied only in a new economic order, a *Grossraumwirtschaft* stretching from the Atlantic to the Urals and controlled by the Germans who would take by force what they needed to sustain themselves and increase their numbers. Racial fantasies, fanatical anti-semitism, economic advantage, strategic necessity, memories of Germany's past greatness and Hitler's restless longing for action combined to make the acquisition of living space the cardinal objective of Nazi foreign policy, vague and ill-defined though the concept remained.[22]

[22] *Grossraumwirtschaft* was a new version of the old *Mitteleuropa* theme of First World War fame. It attracted monopoly capitalist support but is not to be equated with the so-called 'New Order' which had a specifically National Socialist colouration. Cf. A. Milward, 'French Labour and the German economy, 1942–1945: an essay on the nature of the Fascist New Order', *Econ. H. R.* XXIII, 1970.

CHAPTER TWO

The Initial Stages, 1933-1934

WHEN Hitler was appointed chancellor on 30 January 1933 contemporaries did not realize that a new era in German history had begun. Whatever cheering Nazis thought as they stood outside the chancellery, many sober observers supposed that their leader had finally come to terms with the Establishment. The atmosphere of backstairs intrigue surrounding his accession to power in a presidential cabinet seemed to justify this interpretation. And in the next few weeks Hitler encouraged the impression by posing as a man of moderation concerned only to unite the people for the tasks of peaceful reconstruction. The outside world did not know that on 3 February, only four days after his appointment, Hitler made it clear at a private meeting that he was still the radical agitator of old and was as determined as ever to pursue a dynamic foreign policy.

From the outset Hitler intended to secure absolute power and destroy the Weimar system. In the hope of winning an absolute majority at the polls Hitler persuaded the cabinet to agree to new elections. Before he could exploit the new situation to the full, he had to be sure of the army. For, contemptuous though he was of generals as a class, he had always respected military power. So when General von Blomberg, the new minister of war and an ardent Nazi, invited Hitler to address the local army commanders he accepted at once.

After dinner he harangued the assembled officers on the tasks facing the government. As usual he deliberately exaggerated difficulties in order to impress his audience and to give full rein to his longing for radical steps. There was, he insisted, no prospect of an immediate improvement in the economic situation. A renewed export drive was pointless. Production exceeded demand all over the world and Germany's old customers were developing their own markets – not that Hitler was keen on increasing German dependence on 'Jewish-dominated' world markets.

Grudgingly he conceded that resettlement schemes might help reduce unemployment but this would take time and could be no more than a partial solution because the real problem was the lack of adequate living space. He concluded that Germany's economic prospects would brighten only when she recovered her old power in the world. That was the government's immediate task. At home pacifism, Marxism and that 'cancerous growth, democracy' would be stamped out. The German people must learn that ceaseless struggle was the only thing that could save them, and that rearmament was the essential prerequisite for Germany's political resurrection. When Germany recovered her old power, she might find new export markets – though this prospect clearly did not attract him – but probably best of all would be 'the conquest of land in the east and its ruthless Germanisation'.[1] Nothing had changed since the Landsberg days. Nine years later he was attemping to explain Germany's economic crisis in terms of a wholly irrelevant living space theory, making it abundantly clear that he believed in a forcible solution of Germany's economic problems.

Some generals were admittedly alarmed by the tone of the speech. But even they shrugged it off in the end as sound and fury signifying nothing. More reassuring were Hitler's emphatic promises to rearm on a large scale, re-introduce conscription, uphold the non-partisan role of the army and establish an authoritarian state in which the military would enjoy their old privileged position. Hitler returned to the Chancellery well pleased with his reception and confident that he need not fear opposition from the army.

Talk of immediate rearmament was not idle chatter. When plans for a reservoir in Upper Silesia were discussed in cabinet on 8 February, Hitler demanded that priority treatment be given to the armed forces for the next four to five years. Measures for economic recovery must be geared to rearmament because Germany's standing in the world was 'decisively conditioned', in Hitler's opinion, by the strength of her army. Blomberg supported Hitler and the entire cabinet finally agreed to give priority to military expansion in the 1933 budget.

[1] T. Vogelsang (ed.) 'Neue Dokumente zur Geschichte der Reichswehr 1930–1933', *VFZ*, 2, 1954, p. 435; note the similarity with *Hitler's Secret Book*, p. 106.

Before the Nazis came to power Germany was beginning to recover from the worst of the depression. The preceding chancellors, Papen and Schleicher, both recognized the need for some reflation of the economy. Funds were appropriate for public works but neither chancellor had time to implement these plans. On 1 February Hitler, with an eye on the elections, announced two ambitious four-year plans, the first to save the farmer, the other to reduce unemployment. In fact, the Nazis had no panacea for the crisis. All they did was implement the so-called 'immediate programme' of Schleicher's government. What was specifically 'National Socialist' was the marked shift of emphasis towards quasi-military projects in accordance with the principle enunciated by Hitler on 8 February. In June, after discussions with industry, the long-awaited Plan was announced. This combined public works with tax concessions and government subsidies designed to stimulate a revival of private industry. Further measures followed in September. One of the best known outside Germany was the building of the *Reichsautobahnen*, a scheme first mooted in the 1920s, which kept thousands of young men employed for the next six years on the construction of 7,000 kilometres of motor road. This is an excellent example of a multi-purpose measure which helped reduce unemployment (though not until 1934 did it really bite), served as an advertisement for the regime abroad and contributed significantly to Germany's military preparations. No doubt a primary motive behind all these measures was, as Hitler admitted, the sheer political necessity of making inroads into the vast army of unemployed before the winter. But not at the expense of rearmament. Only after Blomberg assured him that sufficient funds were available for military expansion, was Hitler prepared to concentrate on reducing unemployment. Within a year the unemployment average fell from 4·8 millions to 2·7 millions, a success story which greatly encouraged Hitler and led contemporaries to suppose, erroneously, that the Nazis knew from the beginning how to handle the economy.

Large-scale rearmament could not be financed out of the budget, as Hitler quickly realized. The 1932 budget deficit amounted to 900 million *RM* and tax receipts were still shrinking. Funds could not be raised in the money market at a time of acute depression, still less from foreign banks and investors. When Hitler approached the *Reichsbank* in March 1933, its president, Luther, an orthodox financier of the old school, listened sceptically to Hitler's grandiose plans and offered the derisory sum of 100 million *RM* (the maximum which the *Reichsbank* was permitted to advance to governments). Whereupon Hitler promptly sacked Luther and replaced him by Hjalmar Schacht, a well-known financier and enthusiastic admirer of the Führer, who promised, as a condition of appointment, to place the full resources of the bank at the government's disposal.

Schacht's appointment inaugurated a new era in German finance characterized by bold and controversial measures. In some respects he was less of an innovator than he claimed to be. Deficit financing, for example, was not his invention. He simply continued the policies of Papen and Schleicher both of whom planned to stimulate stagnant production with injections of government credit. Schacht's *Mefo* bills, like Schleicher's *Arbeitsbeschaffungswechsel*, were in effect bills of exchange accepted by government contractors and banks and discounted by the *Reichsbank*.[2] *Mefo* bills, like *Arbeitsbeschaffungswechsel* but unlike promissory notes, were prolonged beyond the original ninety days (up to five years) and so acted as a form of short-term credit. Once the money market had recovered, *Mefo* bills earning 4 per cent interest became a desirable investment which attracted fallow capital as Schacht had hoped. Out of a total of 1,200 million bills issued between 1933 and 1938, 6,000 million were, in fact, taken up by the market.

What was new was Schacht's willingness to give virtually unlimited credit to the government. Without these vast sums rearmament on the scale Hitler desired would not have been possible. Of course, Schacht had been too closely associated with currency stabilization in 1924 not to appreciate the dangers inherent in a credit operation on this massive scale. Moreover, unlike previous credit notes, *Mefo* bills were largely used to finance rearmament, i.e. to create unproductive capital goods.[3] For this reason the principles of sound public finance have always

[2] *Mefo* bills so-called after *Metall-Forschungsgesellschaft A.G.*, a dummy corporation formed in May 1933 by four armament firms with the blessing of the defence ministry and on the understanding that the state assumed liability for its debts. This overcame the legal prohibition on the discounting of government bills by the *Reichsbank*.

[3] Although *Mefo* bills financed only 20 per cent of total rearmament in 1934–9, they accounted for 50 per cent of arms expenditure in 1934–5.

required that in the long term armaments be paid for out of taxes and loans. Otherwise the danger of inflation is considerable. No doubt Schacht intended to halt the issue of *Mefo* bills and redeem them when the productive capacity of the country was fully stretched. And indeed by the spring of 1938 taxation and government loans had replaced *Mefo* bills as a means of financing rearmament. Unfortunately, when the redemption date for the first bills approached, Schacht was rapidly losing what influence he had with Hitler. In the end Schacht agreed to further credits of 300 million *RM* in 1937 despite growing disquiet in the *Reichsbank*. Further concessions followed in 1938 going far beyond the bounds of financial prudence. It is an open question whether Schacht's failure was due to fear of offending Hitler or simply because he did not fully realize then, as he did after the war, how precarious the financial situation was. At all events the result was that Germany found herself on the high road to inflation once again. Still, it would be most unfair to blame Schacht wholly for this. The very high rate of government expenditure and the collapse of the wages and prices policy by 1938 were more important causes of general inflation, as will be seen later, and over these Schacht had virtually no control.

The only reason why the highly unstable financial situation after 1936 was not obvious to the general public was because the government took great care to shroud the entire operation of deficit financing in a veil of secrecy. Hitler cared little about the intricacies of high finance – the monetary system was a closed book to him, as Schacht observed – but he was too astute an operator not to appreciate the dangers of overt inflation; any repetition of the disastrous inflation of 1923 would seriously undermine confidence in the regime and must be avoided at all costs. So from the earliest days government agencies deliberately concealed expenditure figures. *Mefo* bills differed from other credit notes only in this respect that from the start every effort was made to keep the entire operation a close secret, on the whole very effectively. This was not just a clever camouflage to hide rearmament from the outside world – though this factor should not be overlooked. Even when rearmament was being carried out quite openly, expenditure figures remained a secret because the Nazis clearly feared to reveal the massive proportions of total government spending.

After the war Schacht maintained that the creation of work places had been as important an objective as rearmament. Investment in armaments had been part of a pump-priming operation to mop up unemployment and set the wheels of industry turning again as quickly as possible, so his defence ran. That is totally unconvincing. For one thing, rearmament continued long after the pump-priming stage. And even at the Nuremberg Trial Schacht made no secret of the importance he had ascribed to rearmament in his overall strategy. He believed that Germany's economic weakness was the root cause of the world depression. World recovery was dependent on German recovery. Like Hitler, he believed that economic recovery was a by-product of political resurgence. Only when Germany again possessed a sizeable army would she be able to play a leading role in Europe once more and recover her colonies (while agreeing with Hitler that Germany's living space was inadequate, Schacht thought that the solution lay in overseas possessions not in eastward expansion). What Schacht did not realize – at least before 1938 – because of his incredible political naïveté was that Hitler fully intended to use the army, if he had to, to realize his imperialist ambitions. Schacht was rightly acquitted on the charge of conspiracy to wage aggressive warfare. But the fact remains that he co-operated wholeheartedly with Hitler in building up Germany's armed forces and cannot, therefore, escape a very substantial share of moral responsibility for the final outcome.

The Treaty of Versailles severely limited the size of Germany's armed forces. She was permitted a small professional army of 100,000 men to preserve order at home but was forbidden to manufacture tanks, gas, military aircraft and submarines. Consequently when Hitler came to power the *Reichswehr* consisted of a mere ten divisions, seven infantry and three cavalry. These were supplemented by illegal *Grenzschutzverbände*, bands of volunteers about 45,000 men in all, who were expected to delay an enemy until the regular army was mobilised. Despite a good deal of secret rearmament from 1920 onwards, Germany was still in an extremely weak position. In 1932 the troop office, the forerunner of the army general staff, believed that effective resistance to a combined Franco-Polish attack would not be possible before 1944. Some progress had been made towards the creation of an airforce where preparations stretched back to the end of the First World War. Even so in 1933 Germany possessed only about eighty aircraft and 450 flying personnel. The navy had not even attained the levels permitted by treaty and most of the existing craft were of pre-war vintage.

As Germany started to regain some of her old influence in the early 1930s, all three branches of the armed forces drew up plans for expansion. The navy envisaged modest increases over a six-year period through even so it proposed to exceed the Versailles limit only in respect of smaller craft. The army plan approved by Schleicher was more ambitious; between April 1933 and March 1938 the army planned to expand from seven to twenty-one divisions thus enabling Germany to put 300,000 men in the field when fully mobilized. However, for various reasons little could be done to make a practical start on these plans before the Nazis came to power.

The Nazis had no specific plans for military expansion. At first Hitler seems to have toyed with the idea of pushing ahead with rearmament at breakneck speed regardless of foreign reactions.[4] He soon decided against this, and did what he had done over the economic situation: he took over the plans of the previous government. Temporarily at any rate rearmament was to proceed on the basis of Schleicher's plan leaving undecided the final peace-time strength of the armed forces. There was to be no shortage of finance. In the spring of 1933 before turning his attention to economic recovery, Hitler promised army, navy and airforce ample funds for the next five years.[5] Rearmament in 1933 took the form of unspectacular but essential reorganization work to create the framework for rapid expansion later on. No immediate improvement in Germany's strategic position was possible—indeed reorganization tended temporarily to weaken the fighting potential of the army. Its effective strength remained practically unchanged and in an emergency could do little more than offer localized resistance, as Blomberg admitted frankly in his directive to the armed forces in October 1933.[6] The same was true of navy and airforce.

[4] H. Rauschning, *Hitler speaks* (London, 1939), p. 157.

[5] Military expenditure in 1933 amounted to 1,900 million *RM* compared with 800 millions in 1932. This represented an increase from 1 per cent to 3 per cent of the GNP.

[6] The fact that Blomberg was ready to offer hopeless resistance to foreign invaders speaks volumes for the new spirit of the army.

What was not clear in 1933 was the precise form the new German army would take. At first Hitler was much preoccupied with the future role in the Third Reich of the Brownshirts, the Nazis' private army led by ex-*Reichswehr* captain Ernst Roehm. Throughout 1933 Roehm's followers, who had borne the heat of the day in many a bloody street battle, remained bitterly resentful of the Führer's flirtation with the Establishment. The Brownshirt legions, numbering one million activists, kept Germany in a state of suspense with their talk of a second 'socialist' revolution to supersede the national revolution. To destroy the power of the 'reactionaries', Roehm planned to replace the *Reichswehr* with a huge revolutionary army permeated with the National Socialist spirit and under his control. The generals, who had nothing but contempt for the Brownshirts, were resolutely opposed to such schemes and utterly determined to preserve the officer corps from contamination. The issue was of crucial importance to Hitler. A peoples' militia controlled by Roehm did not attract him; war was too serious a matter to leave to freebooters and adventurers. When it came to the crunch in June 1934 Hitler had to side with the professionals against the amateurs. That does not mean that Hitler automatically endorsed the generals' views on the future shape of the army. Reichenau's plan for an elite army of 400,000 supplemented by a Brownshirt militia would certainly have produced a first-class fighting force. But Hitler wanted the best of both worlds: a well-equipped and powerful mass army trained and led by professional soldiers but under his personal control, not Roehm's. A professionally-led mass army was Hitler's ideal. Rapid expansion would impress the outside world and shift the balance of power back to Berlin more quickly. Expansion would shake to pieces the socially-exclusive officers corps, which Hitler detested just as much as Roehm, and would turn the army into a reliable National Socialist institution. Finally, a mass army was an educative force, 'the school of the German people in arms', an essential propaganda instrument for developing the martial spirit of the nation. Until the future of the Brownshirts had been decided, the shape of the new army could not be decided, therefore the pace of rearmament was to some extent slowed down.

'The first task of German foreign policy', Hitler stated in the *Secret Book*, 'is primarily the creation of conditions which make possible the resurrection of a German army. For only then will the peoples' vital needs be able to find their practical representation.'[7] It was abundantly clear to him that this task could be accomplished only if the Great Powers did not regard German rearmament as a threat to their vital interests. On 3 February Hitler warned the local army commanders that the rearmament period would be a most dangerous time; if there were any statesmen left in France they would surely attack Germany while there was still time. Alarmed talk in the French press in the spring of 1933 and demands for action in the Chamber of Deputies should Germany violate the Versailles Treaty seemed to confirm Hitler's worst fears. A cautious foreign policy operating strictly within the limits of German military power was absolutely mandatory. Talking to the Nazi *Bürgermeister* of Hamburg in March 1933, Hitler summed his policy up succinctly: the sabre-rattling heard in some nationalist circles was quite inappropriate as long as Germany was unarmed; she must seek a truce with the other powers for at least six years simply because she needed a period of peace and quiet and economic growth to become strong again.[8] Reviewing the first five years of power in a secret speech to journalists in November 1938, Hitler remarked that he had been obliged to speak of peace for a decade in order to obtain armaments 'which were an essential prerequisite . . . for the next step.'[9] From the start Hitler's policy was rooted in deliberate deception. Public declarations of Germany's desire for peace were tactical manœuvres designed to allay doubts and fears about his intentions and ensure that rearmament proceeded without hindrance; in no way did these pacific protestations correspond with his secret longing to destroy the status quo as quickly as possible.

A pacific foreign policy served other ends. Much as Hitler detested 'traditional' diplomacy and suspected foreign office officials and diplomats of disloyalty to the regime, he could not

[7] *Hitler's Secret Book*, p. 85.

[8] Cf. Blomberg to army commanders 2 February 1934: 'Chancellor's thought is: secure the peace for a number of years so that Reich can be reconstructed and armed forces rebuilt . . .' Quoted in G. Meinck, *Hitler und die deutsche Aufrüstung 1933–39* (Wiesbaden, 1959), p. 81.

[9] W. Treue, 'Hitlers Rede vor der deutschen Presse 10 November 1938', *VFZ*, 6, 1958, p. 182.

do without them.[10] The establishment in April of the *Aussen-politisches Amt*, a Nazi party agency under Alfred Rosenberg dabbling in foreign affairs, was a deliberate attempt to clear the way for drastic changes in the diplomatic service later on. But it did virtually nothing to reduce dependence on the professionals for the immediate future. In fact, Hitler's suspicions were largely unfounded. The foreign office and the diplomatic corps whole-heartedly approved of the nationalist policy which the Nazis propagated in public. It cannot be emphasized too strongly that solid support from foreign office and army command were the foundations on which Hitler's subsequent successes rested. Foreign office officials made the same mistake as the generals. They discounted Hitler's racial fantasies and living space chatter, and persuaded themselves, despite ominous signs to the contrary, that *Anschluss* with Austria, frontier revision in the east and the recovery of Danzig were his real aims. Fears that the chancellor might be tempted into reckless enterprises were further diminished when he conformed to the ritual exercises of con-ventional diplomacy and deported himself on state occasions with surprising skill and moderation, a considerable achievement for a man with no knowledge of foreign languages and virtually no experience of the outside world. The foreign office was lulled into a false sense of security by Hitler's deliberately misleading remark that he knew nothing of foreign policy and that his task for the next four years was to make Germany National Socialist. 'Only then could he bother about foreign policy. Apart from that the foreign office was an institution governed by long-established traditions. Finally he had to have regard for what went on above.'[11] The reference to Hindenburg points to another factor making for stability and moderation in the early months of power. Though constantly chafing at the need to humour the octogenarian presi-dent, Hitler understood perfectly well that until he was firmly established in power and had the army on a short rein Hinden-burg's wish for continuity of policy must be respected. That was

[10] In conversation with Rosenberg in May 1934 Hitler described the foreign office as a 'nest of conspirators'. He regretted that he had ever allowed Hinden-burg to control foreign policy and the army. Thanks to Blomberg the army was all right but not the foreign policy. H. G. Seraphim, *Das politische Tagebuch Alfred Rosenbergs 1934/35 und 1939/40* (Göttingen-Berlin-Frankfurt, 1956), p. 20.

[11] R. Nadolny, *Mein Beitrag* (Wiesbaden, 1955), p. 130.

probably decisive in the appointment of the foreign minister in February 1933. On the president's insistence Hitler retained the conservative von Neurath instead of appointing his favourite Rosenberg.

The appearance of the German delegation at the newly-opened session of the Disarmament Conference in February was welcomed abroad as a reassuring sign of the continuity of German policy. In reality Hitler knew already that negotiations would be fruitless because the powers could not possibly approve of re-armament on the scale he envisaged. However, a German refusal to attend would only draw attention to his intention to rearm and might even precipitate the preventive war he feared. It seemed safer to go through the motions of negotiation while reserving the right to withdraw when it suited his convenience. That neither Hitler nor Neurath attended any part of the Conference is an indication of the importance they attached to the operation. In March, in a desperate attempt to break the deadlock caused by the clash between the German demand for equality of armaments (in which Hitler did not believe) and French insistence on a security system, MacDonald, the British prime minister, produced a plan containing concrete proposals for arms reductions. After some hesitation Hitler expressed positive interest but only because he wished to avoid assuming responsibility for the breakdown of the conference at that stage. By now mounting criticism of the Nazis' suppression of liberty at home was seriously tarnishing Germany's reputation. In May Hitler delivered a celebrated speech on foreign policy in which he displayed for the first time his uncanny instinct for striking the chords most likely to reassure his critics; dissatisfaction with the Versailles Treaty was cleverly blended with protestations of his abhorrence of war, denials of expansionist ambitions and an affirmation of his willingness to accept general disarmament in principle. Despite the soothing assurances the situation did not improve. Continuing indignation at Nazi excesses coupled with disturbing (and exaggerated) rumours of secret rearmament caused attitudes to harden in the summer of 1933. France was especially worried by the size of the Brownshirt army and in the end insisted upon modification of the MacDonald Plan to test out security arrangements for four years before disarming down to the German level.

Hitler seized on this as a convenient excuse for terminating negotiations in which he had never believed. When France, under pressure from Britain, tried conciliatory tactics, Hitler stiffened the German demands to ensure a speedy breakdown. Neurath and Blomberg fully agreed with Hitler as did practically the entire foreign office. Hindenburg was won over by Hitler's argument that withdrawal from the conference and the League of Nations as well were essential steps on the road to complete equality of status and unrestricted sovereignty. On 13 October Hitler obtained cabinet agreement. Reprisals by the Great Powers were thought most unlikely; Germany's ambassadors in Paris, London and Rome had all discounted the possibility of sanctions. So confident of success was Hitler that no military precautions were taken prior to the announcement on 14 October.

There is no evidence that Hitler needed a foreign success at this moment to allay discontent inside Germany. However, there can be little doubt that the internal situation had a direct bearing on Hitler's decision but for quite different reasons. By the summer of 1933 German democracy had been destroyed, all parties except the Nazis had disappeared and the one-party state was an ugly reality. Left-wing opposition to the Nazis had been stifled with the suppression of the trade union movement while Catholic criticism of the new paganism was muted out of gratitude for the concordat negotiated with the Vatican in July 1933 at Hitler's express command. In short, the first stage of internal consolidation had been successfully accomplished and much more quickly than Hitler expected. It was no longer necessary to move quite so cautiously in foreign affairs especially when, as in the case of withdrawal from Geneva, serious complications, for which Germany was militarily unprepared, were unlikely to arise. The whole episode illustrates excellently the interdependence of internal and external policy.[12] If stability at home encouraged Hitler to act with less restraint abroad, it is equally apparent that success abroad was used to bolster up the regime at home. Germany's withdrawal from Geneva was accompanied by the dissolution of the Reichstag. The new elections on 12 November offered the electorate the choice of voting (or not, depending on

[12] Hitler saw the connection: 'Domestic policy must secure the inner strength of a people so that it can assert itself in the sphere of foreign policy. Hence domestic policy and foreign policy are not only most closely linked but must also mutually complement each other.' *Hitler's Secret Book*, p. 34.

their degree of moral courage) for a one-party list. The Landtage were dissolved and not recalled, a further step towards complete nazification. On 12 November the Germans were asked to approve by plebiscite the government's foreign policy. Ninety-five per cent of the electorate replied in the affirmative, a great propaganda victory for Hitler and a result which, allowing for Nazi irregularities at the polls, reflected widespread support for the 'turning away from the West'. The Nazi expression is an apt one. Hitler had struck the first blow at the international policies of previous governments. After this Germany took no part in international conferences but withdrew gradually from most multilateral agreements into splendid isolation. From this vantage point she concluded whatever bilateral pacts seemed expedient in accordance with the strategy laid down by Hitler in *Mein Kampf.* Finally, though it was not immediately apparent, his successful defiance of the outside world started to tip the balance away from the foreign office and placed the initiative in foreign affairs increasingly in the Führer's hands.

Striking confirmation of Hitler's ascendancy in the field of foreign affairs came in January 1934 when Germany signed a non-aggression pact with Poland. This pact, taken in conjunction with a noticeable cooling-off in Russo-German relations in the summer of 1934, represented a sharp break with past policy. Ties between Russia and Germany stretched far back into the nineteenth century. The collapse of autocracy in Russia and Germany at the end of the First World War failed to alter the basic identity of interest between them. As early as 1922 Weimar Germany concluded economic agreements with Moscow partly to recapture badly-needed markets for German capital goods but mainly because Russia was the natural enemy of Poland and a potential ally against that country. The very existence of Poland was an abomination in German eyes, a constant reminder of defeat. Successive governments refused to recognize the eastern frontier and made no secret of their intention to recover the lost lands. As Poland was a powerful state in the 1920s, relatively speaking, the *Reichswehr* regarded her as a potential danger to Germany. In the spring of 1932 army circles were genuinely alarmed at the possibility of a Polish attack on Silesia. Army apprehension reached a new peak in March 1933 when Polish marines landed on the Westerplatte peninsula, a gesture designed to deter the Nazis from precipitate action in Danzig. There were alarming rumours in the spring that Marshal Pilsudski was seeking French agreement for joint military action against Germany. Such developments underlined the continuing need for the Russian connection. Neurath was in no doubt that 'defence against Poland is possible only if the support of Russia is assured'.[13] Consequently official policy did not change. In May 1933 the Treaty of Berlin was renewed and as late as July Goebbels's propaganda ministry warned the press against direct attacks on Russia.

The one man who thought differently about Germany's eastern policy was Hitler. From the beginning he disliked the foreign office's pro-Russian policy as he explained to Reichenau in 1932.[14] On ideological grounds he opposed ties with the power directing the very 'Marxist revolution' he was stamping out in Germany. Power political considerations were even more important; in 1932 France had persuaded Poland to sign a non-aggression pact with Russia so that the Poles would not be intimidated by the growing power of that state. This, concluded Hitler tortuously, was evidence of 'encirclement' which he was determined to neutralize by some diplomatic coup. By the spring of 1933 he decided that an agreement with Poland was the ideal way of doing this. Since the Westerplatte incident Hitler had restrained the Danzig Nazis and handled Poland with great care, perhaps because he was impressed by her evident determination to resist German encroachments. Relations improved steadily. Disputes between Danzig and Poland were settled satisfactorily. In September negotiations commenced to terminate the eight-year-old tariff war between them. In October Hitler finally made up his mind to seek a non-aggression pact with Poland, possibly influenced by a fear that she might otherwise be tempted by France into military action against Germany when the latter withdrew from the Disarmament Conference. Negotiations commenced in November and in January 1934 the pact was signed. The improvement in relations with Poland was accompanied by a deterioration in Russo-German relations. Admittedly economic and military ties were wearing thin before Hitler came to power. All Hitler did was accelerate the process of disengagement. In

[13] *DGFP*, C, I, no. 142.
[14] T. Vogelsang (ed.) 'Hitlers Brief an Reichenau von 4 December', *VFZ*, 7 1959; cf. R. Nadolny, *op. cit.*, pp. 138, 167.

July 1934 military co-operation finally ceased on the pretext that Russia was becoming too friendly with France.

The Nazis celebrated the Polish pact as a great diplomatic victory. Strategically the French defensive system in the east had been decisively breached and the danger of 'encirclement' averted. No doubt Hitler saw it in this light. Whether he was right to do so is another matter. Far from diminishing the danger of encirclement, it might be argued that Hitler had increased it in the long term. France and Russia were already groping towards an understanding at the end of 1933. The Polish pact could not fail to accelerate Russia's *rapprochement* with the west. In February 1934 Russia ratified her non-aggression pact with France and in September became a member of the League of Nations. In a vain attempt to maintain the Russian connection, Nadolny, the German ambassador in Moscow, warned Hitler in May of the grave dangers of complete isolation. The Führer, irritated by Nadolny's obstinacy, cut him short with the retort that the western powers and Russia were enemies of Germany's will to live. He restated once again his intention of freeing Germany from all international obligations and making her strong militarily and economically so that she could attain her objectives by her own unaided efforts. The pessimistic Nadolny was virtually isolated. One of the most revealing features in the situation was the docility with which an overwhelming majority of foreign office officials, diplomats, army commanders and East Prussian land-owners acquiesced in a policy running counter to their deepest prejudices. That they did this so readily speaks volumes for Hitler's high standing in Establishment circles.

The pact did not seriously inhibit Hitler's freedom of man-œuvre. True, an unavoidable consequence was the abandonment of the traditional Weimar policy of protecting the German minority in Poland. But to Hitler that minority was as expend-able as the German minority in the south Tyrol. Nor had Hitler necessarily abandoned the Polish Germans for ever or given up German claims to Danzig and the Corridor. The Nazi rank-and-file felt instinctively that the pact was a sham and that the Führer would deal with the Poles in his own good time. Up to a point their instincts were correct. Hitler told party leaders in October 1933 that he would sign any treaty to postpone war until he was ready. To Rauschning he explained that the pact had a 'purely temporary significance'.[15] There may have been more to it. As revisionism was not his aim, it followed that hostility to Poland was not an integral part of his strategy. The search for living space, not marginal improvements in existing frontiers, was the real objective and the promised land lay in Russia, not in Poland. So even in 1934 it was not inconceivable that he hoped to win Poland as an ally for war against Russia. He was undoubtedly impressed by fellow dictator Pilsudski and often assured Polish statesmen that their country was 'a last barricade of civilization in the east'.[16] All one can say with certainty is that the pact had served its immediate purpose and the future was left to take care of itself.

A month later Hitler made it abundantly clear that one year in office had not changed his ultimate aims one iota. The conflict between the army and the Brownshirts was moving to a climax in the spring of 1934. In February Roehm sought cabinet approval for the amalgamation of the armed forces, the party's para-military organizations and war veterans' organizations under one ministry. On 28 February at a special conference attended by local army commanders and party leaders Hitler announced his decision: Roehm's plan was rejected, the Brownshirts were relegated to the task of political re-education and the *Reichswehr* was to be the only armed body in Germany. To justify a decision deeply wounding to old comrades, Hitler launched into a *tour d'horizon* full of the usual distortions and alarmist talk. The party had solved the unemployment problem, he boasted – a claim which scarcely carried conviction in the winter of 1933/4. Nevertheless, an economic recession was inevitable in eight years' time. To avoid 'frightful destitution' which would then engulf her, Germany would be obliged to acquire living space to accommodate her surplus population. Opposition from the the western powers was certain; therefore, 'short decisive blows to the west and then to the east would be necessary'.[17] A Roehm-type militia would be of little use. What Germany must have was

[15] H. Rauschning, *op. cit.*, p. 123.

[16] K. Lipski, *Diplomat in Berlin 1933–1939* (New York–London, 1968), p. 125.

[17] R. O'Neill, *The German Army and the Nazi Party* (London, 1966), pp. 40–1. By 'west' he meant only France for at this time he still believed that Britain would become his partner and allow France to be destroyed in return for a guarantee of the British Empire.

a powerful peoples' army based on the *Reichswehr*, ready for defensive action in five years and for offensive action in eight years; for the first time Hitler had laid down a 'timetable' for attaining his objectives. Field-Marshal von Weichs noted that the soldiers at the conference were relieved by the unequivocal declaration in their favour and chose to ignore the warlike prophecies. Only later, as Weichs ruefully admits, was it apparent that Hitler 'had set forth his complete foreign policy programme and already intimated the possibility of aggressive war'.[18]

Hitler's impatience with the pace of rearmament probably played some part in the decision to break with Geneva; the prospect of a disarmament convention with arms controls inhibiting German progress heightened his resolve to be done with negotiation. The Great Powers failed to act in concert against Germany. For a brief moment France thought of imposing an agreement on Hitler until Britain refused to co-operate. Like Italy she preferred direct negotiation with Germany. The ensuing conversations dragged on throughout the winter of 1933/4 and confirmed Hitler's opinion that he could go ahead without fear of reprisals. His sharp eye for power realities prompted him to remark to close associates in January 1934 that even France would tolerate German rearmament unofficially provided no fuss was made about it. The Polish pact removed any lingering doubts. On 1 February when Freiherr von Fritsch was appointed commander-in-chief of the army Hitler ordered him to create a strong army as quickly as possible. On 28 February, as we have seen already, the army commanders were informed of Hitler's 'timetable'.

As the struggle with the Brownshirts deepened, the army command came round to the view that rapid expansion was the best way of strengthening the *Reichswehr* against Roehm's followers. Furthermore, whilst the generals resented the Polish pact they were quick to appreciate its strategic significance. Schleicher's plan, taken over by the Nazis, envisaged a wartime army of twenty-one divisions. In December 1933 the troop office submitted plans for a peacetime army of twenty-one divisions by 1937. In January 1934 a secret law reduced the period of service from twelve years to one year, an essential step for obtaining the reserves a vastly expanded regular army would need to face the

[18] *The German Army and the Nazi Party*, p. 41.

French. In April 1934 the French played into Hitler's hands by dramatically breaking off the sagging disarmament negotiations on the grounds that Germany was not in earnest, and therefore France must look to her defences. Hitler knew that he had a free hand to do as he pleased. While Germany rearmed she could rely on Italian goodwill and British and American passivity.

In April 1934 when the new army reform became operative, the *Reichswehr* recruited 50–70,000 men. Hitler was still not satisfied with the progress being made and insisted that the organizational framework for twenty-one divisions be created by the autumn, i.e. three years ahead of schedule. Objections from General Beck, head of the troop office, who expressed anxiety about foreign reactions as well as the technical effects of over-hasty rearmament, were curtly dismissed. By the summer of 1934 rearmament was gathering pace. In October another 70,000 recruits joined the *Reichswehr* bringing the total up to 240,000 men. To this total should be added 200,000 policemen re-organized, armed and trained as infantrymen. When finally re-incorporated in the *Reichswehr* in 1935 they comprised three divisions. The acceleration in the tempo of rearmament is well illustrated by the growth of the airforce. In the summer of 1933 Goering planned to have 1,000 aircraft by 1935. In July 1934 a new plan envisaged 4,000 aircraft by September 1935 and by the end of 1934, 2,000 of these had materialized. Whatever doubts some generals harboured about the wisdom of accelerated expansion, their confidence in Germany's military capabilities was restored. Even the critical Beck admitted in September 1934 that the military situation had altered radically. Blomberg's directive of October 1933 was accordingly modified. The objective of war was to be the defeat of the enemy as in the old days. Owing to the present state of armament the *Reichswehr* could only play a predominantly defensive role in war but a limited switch to the offensive was not impossible provided expansion continued.

Germany's Achilles heel in two world wars was her dependence on world markets for essential raw materials and certain food imports. No amount of propaganda about racial superiority could alter the hard fact that Germany in 1929 imported 80 per cent of her iron ore (half from Sweden), 85 per cent of her petrol, fuel oil and other petroleum requirements, most of her aluminium and all her nickel, molybdenum, chrome, tungsten and natural rubber; in short, most of the essential constituents of a modern war machine. In addition 20 per cent of her food was imported. By the beginning of 1934 Germany's economic recovery had created balance of payments problems. As the economy revived, consumer demand grew and this coupled with rearmament sharply increased imports. Unfortunately exports had fallen steadily since 1929 partly because devaluation in other countries made German exports dearer, and partly because tariff walls and quotas made it difficult to secure markets. A favourable trade balance of 667 million *RM* in 1933 was transformed into a deficit of 284 million *RM* in 1934. By the end of the year only 80 millions remained in the gold reserves. In June the import quota system inherited from Bruening collapsed completely, and the country was threatened with widespread unemployment. Germany was brought up sharply against the fact of her dependence on international markets at the very moment when Hitler accelerated rearmament. As Kurt Schmitt, the minister of economics, had offended big business by his opposition to cartels, and the generals because of his opposition to the production of synthetic oil, Hitler dismissed him and strengthened Schacht's position still further by making him the new economics minister.

In an attempt to satisfy the demands of the military for increased raw material imports, Schacht adopted new policies. Firstly, he imposed an absolute moratorium on Germany's foreign debts to stop the outflow of precious foreign exchange as interest payments. Secondly, he introduced the so-called New Plan which greatly extended and strengthened existing state control over foreign exchange and imports.[19] With these new controls Schacht succeeded temporarily in overcoming the crisis. Drastic reductions of inessential imports of manufactured goods together with determined efforts to boost exports – or at least to offset the effect of foreign devaluation on existing exports – did the trick. Manipulation of 'blocked marks', elaborate clearing arrangements and disguised export subsidies were some of the 'Schachtian devilries', as one economist called them, which

---

[19] The plan failed to satisfy autarky-minded Nazis entrenched in the ministry of agriculture who demanded the cutting of imports to an absolute minimum and the replacement of quotas by extensive barter agreements.

helped to turn the balance of payments deficit into a surplus by 1935.[20]

One consequence of Schacht's policies was a significant movement of trade away from Western Europe and the USA towards the Balkans and Latin America. This reflected the qualitative change occurring in German trade where manufactured imports were declining sharply and food and raw material imports increasing. Latin America and the Balkans attracted Germany because both areas possessed large surpluses of primary produce which could not be absorbed in world markets. Secondly, these backward areas would accept German goods in exchange whereas Western Europe and the USA would not. Thirdly, in the case of the Balkans it made political and strategic sense to trade with neighbouring countries which would become dependent on the German economy. Schacht set out to do just this by deliberately creating unfavourable trade balances with Balkan countries and by encouraging them to produce the minerals and oil Germany needed and for which these countries could not easily find alternative markets. In return Germany offered them machinery instead of consumer goods which were in short supply as a result of deliberate Nazi policy. Schacht's methods were aggressive and sometimes none too honest as, for example, with Yugoslavia in 1936. He offered to take 60 per cent of Yugoslavia's grain harvest at a price 30 per cent above market prices, a favourite German device for eliminating competitors. The Yugoslavian government agreed and made advance payments to their farmers. Meanwhile Germany sold a large part of the grain in Rotterdam and London at world prices and with the foreign exchange purchased raw materials for rearmament. Yugoslavia was then informed that Germany could not pay in foreign exchange but would supply goods instead. However, when the Yugoslavian delegation visited Germany it found manufacturers reluctant to supply heavy machinery because the Nazis insisted on priority for rearmament needs. Such cavalier treatment did not endear Balkan clients to Germany. While German economic influence in the Balkans grew steadily from 1934 to 1936, its importance should not be overestimated. By 1937 there was widespread disillusionment with Germany's inability to deliver the goods or supply the capital

[20] R. F. Harrod, *The Life and Times of John Maynard Keynes* (London, 1951), p. 512.

desperately needed by her Balkan customers. They quickly grew tired of having to accept typewriters, aspirins and mouth organs in return for their grain, and refused to allow Germany to run up new debts. By 1938 the German import surplus with the Balkans had vanished completely. If an economic recession had not intervened in 1937, western business interests might easily have supplanted the Germans. Only after the *Anschluss*, and especially after Munich, did German economic influence, and the political influence which went with it, become a dominant factor in the area, another instance of economic influence following political conquests rather than preceding them.

By the end of 1934 Hitler was firmly established in power. The complete nazification of Germany was well advanced; the Brown-shirt problem had been resolved by ruthless measures which turned them into a docile instrument of the Führer's; and Schacht's wizardry had smoothed the path for accelerated rearmament. Abroad, however, Germany remained virtually isolated in a hostile and unfriendly world. One of the reasons for wide-spread suspicion of Germany was the course of events in Austria.

Austria occupied a special place in the Führer's affections. His formative years were spent in Linz and Vienna. On the first page of *Mein Kampf* he committed the Nazis to the union of Austria and Germany. Once in power he seems to have thought that he could bring Austria under his wing in the very near future by a process of gradual assimilation with the help of the indigenous Austrian Nazi movement. His treatment of Austria was, therefore, curiously unrelated to the rest of his foreign policy. In the main he pursued a cautious and restrained foreign policy corresponding to power realities and German military strength, moving forward only when no resistance was to be expected. Not so with Austria, where he bullied and intimidated the Dollfuss government with reckless disregard for international repercussions. One can only assume that he expected the Great Powers to treat an *Anschluss* as a purely internal matter and not as a violation of treaty obligations. The foreign office, on the other hand, though approving wholeheartedly of Hitler's objective, was fearful of foreign complications and warned against a forward policy. For that reason and because he wanted to be free of foreign office 'interference', Hitler preferred to rely on party officials as intermediaries. His choice was Theo Habicht, Reichstag member and provincial inspector of the Austrian Nazis, who was sent to Vienna as the Führer's special emissary in May 1933.

Since 1926 the Austrian Nazis had been an integral part of the German movement, in receipt of financial aid from Berlin and supported by Goebbels's propaganda machine. Confident in the spring of 1933 that the Führer would not tolerate Chancellor Dollfuss much longer, the Austrian Nazis intensified their disruptive activities. Relations between Austria and Germany deteriorated. In May Hitler imposed a prohibitive tax on visas to Austria in the confident expectation that a decline in tourism would bring Dollfuss down and precipitate new elections; this would lead to the Nazification of Austria obviating the need for open *Anschluss*.

The strategem misfired. Dollfuss retaliated in kind by requiring travellers to Germany to purchase visas. After further disturbances in June, the Austrian Nazis were banned and Habicht expelled from Austria. An angry Führer turned the propaganda machine on full blast. Over the radio and in leaflets dropped by aeroplane the Austrian people was urged to overthrow the 'crumbling' Dollfuss regime. Chancellor Dollfuss appealed to Britain and France for assistance. Italy, too, was alarmed by Nazi intrigues in her Danubian sphere of influence. Britain and France protested in Berlin about Nazi excesses while Mussolini, much to Hitler's chagrin, asked Germany independently for assurances that an *Anschluss* was not contemplated. For once Neurath was able to persuade Hitler to moderate his bellicose campaign. Reluctantly he ordered Habicht to exercise more restraint, stopped aerial propaganda and withdrew the Austrian Legion (a para-military organization composed of Nazi refugees from Austria) from the Bavarian frontier.

In the autumn Dollfuss decided that agreement with Germany was essential to avoid complete dependence on Italy. But unofficial approaches quickly revealed Hitler's complete intransigence. In return for a guarantee of Austria's independence, he demanded the raising of the ban on the Austrian Nazis and half the seats in the cabinet for their leaders with the discredited Habicht as vice-chancellor. While Dollfuss hesitated to refuse impossible terms, the Austrian *Heimwehr*, a pro-Italian para-military body, made his mind up for him by vetoing further discussions with Germany. After that Dollfuss became the prisoner of the Italians and at their request crushed the Austrian Socialists in February 1934.

Only in the spring of 1934 did Hitler begin to lose hope of acquiring Austria in the near future. When Britain, France and Italy solemnly guaranteed Austrian independence in February, Hitler ordered Habicht to avoid the use of force and to desist from direct attacks on the Dollfuss regime. To Neurath the Führer commented that he desired neither Nazification nor *Anschluss*; the Dollfuss regime was obviously stronger since its suppression of socialism and would not now be interested in coming to terms with the Nazis; the latter must avoid the use of force until the situation changed and concentrate instead on long-term propaganda to increase party membership. In April Hitler declared to Neurath and others that he was 'quite ready to write off Austria for some years to come and hand her over to economic fertilization by Italy'.[21]

The dramatic events in July 1934 arose at least in part out of the fact that Hitler's influence over the Austrian Nazis was limited. They had been there before Hitler and while willingly availing themselves of German aid, saw no reason why they should abandon hope of an early *Anschluss*. After a pause in the spring, Nazi agitation in Austria recommenced. It culminated in an uprising in Vienna on 25 July which was easily suppressed but not before the 'pocket chancellor', Dollfuss, had been brutally murdered. Whether Hitler was privy to the plot is uncertain. Goering at the Nuremberg Trial suggested that Habicht was the real villain of the piece having hoodwinked Hitler into believing that the Austrian army was ready to overthrow Dollfuss. In those circumstances Hitler promised political support for an Austrian Nazi uprising. The 'whole army' turned out to be a lone *SS* unit which hoped to carry the army with it in a putsch. On the other hand, the latest authority in the field believes that while direct evidence of Hitler's complicity is lacking, he was too powerful a figure not to have known and must have approved of the plot.[22]

---

[21] *DGFP*, C, II, no. 393. But he was unwilling to say this to Mussolini in so many words let alone in writing. Nor did he think Italian attempts to revive Trieste and Fiume would succeed.

[22] G. Weinberg, *The foreign policy of Hitler's Germany. Diplomatic Revolution in Europe, 1933–1936* (Chicago and London .1970), pp. 102–4.

Whatever the truth of the matter – and reasonable doubt will probably always remain – the appearance of four Italian divisions on the Brenner Pass sharpened Hitler's perception wonderfully.[23] The hard fact was that the German army was unable to under-write the failure of Austrian hotheads and German policy changed abruptly. Hitler had to accept that an *Anschluss* was impossible until the international situation changed, i.e. until Germany was strong enough to change it. Meanwhile conciliation was the order of the day. Hindenburg sent a telegram of condolence to the Austrian president; Habicht fell from favour; the Austrian Nazi headquarters in Munich were closed; the Austrian Nazis were ordered to behave with more restraint; finally, a masterly stroke, Vice-Chancellor von Papen was dispatched to Vienna as special envoy to improve Austro-German relations and prepare the way for *Anschluss* at a later date.

[23] 'We are faced with a second Sarajevo' was his dramatic comment; F. von Papen, *Memoirs* (London, 1952), p. 338.

CHAPTER THREE

The Struggle for Control of the German Economy, 1936

AT the beginning of 1935 Germany still remained virtually isolated in Europe. The progress of illegal rearmament, stories of systematic repression at home and the alarming episode of the Austrian putsch did nothing to inspire confidence in the Nazis. But it would be wrong to suppose that Hitler was unduly worried about isolation. In conversation with Goering in January 1935 the Führer revealed that he was already contemplating some move over armaments in the near future. When Britain, anxious to prevent a new arms race, put out feelers to Germany in February Hitler was encouraged by what he interpreted as further evidence of weakness. Negotiations with Britain and France were a useful smokescreen and accordingly Hitler made encouraging noises about the Anglo-French proposal for an air pact. Rather to Hitler's surprise, Britain was eager to negotiate at once and the foreign secretary, Sir John Simon, prepared to visit Berlin. As the German cabinet had just approved a secret decree on the airforce on 26 February with the intention of an early public announcement, Simon's visit would be acutely embarrassing. A pretext for delaying the conversations presented itself with the publication on 4 March of the British White Paper on Defence, a document which roundly condemned Nazi military preparations. On 9 March in an interview with Ward Price of the *Daily Mail* Goering revealed the existence of a German airforce. The announcement aroused so little surprise that the powers did not even bother to lodge formal protests.

Perhaps this encouraged Hitler to go further than originally intended. He was already impatient to start on the build-up of manpower reserves without which armies cannot face war.[1]

[1] In January 1932 Hitler told German industrialists that whether Germany had an army of 100,000, 200,000 or 300,000 was not significant; what mattered was whether she had eight million reservists or not; N. Baynes, *op. cit.*, I, pp. 816–17.

Reserves depended upon the introduction of conscription which the generals expected Hitler to announce in the autumn. On 10 March Hitler learnt that France intended to increase the period of compulsory service from one to two years and reduce the age of enlistment in order to neutralize the effects of a falling birth rate. The Führer withdrew to the Berghof to brood over the problem. On 14 March he informed his adjutant, Colonel Hossbach, that he intended to re-introduce conscription and expand the army – he accepted without question the figure of thirty-six peacetime divisions which, so Hossbach told him, was the army's new target. But Hitler consulted neither Blomberg nor Fritsch nor Neurath beforehand, preferring to keep army command and foreign office in the dark until the last minute, possibly to emphasize that since Hindenburg's death he was supreme master accountable to no one.

When Hossbach informed Blomberg of the Führer's decision, the minister of war was horrified. At a hastily-convened meeting of ministers chaired by Hitler Blomberg expressed deep concern at possible foreign reaction. In contrast, the civilian ministers sided with Hitler against Blomberg. Characteristically, the weak and compliant minister of war had suppressed his doubts by the next day. The decision to expand the army caused more widespread concern in military circles. Fritsch probably spoke for the entire high command on 16 March when he stressed the dangers of overhasty expansion and observed that it would take several years to bring the army up to the new strength, an opinion which Hitler brushed aside contemptuously.

When the re-introduction of conscription was announced on 16 March Britain, France and Italy protested solemnly at a unilateral breach of treaty obligations. Their foreign secretaries assembled at Stresa in April to express collective regret. Finally, the Council of the League of Nations denounced Germany's action and established a committee to consider the implication of sanctions on offending states – but only on future offenders. In short, they behaved exactly as Hitler expected. The *Aussenpolitisches Amt* and other intelligence agencies, on which Hitler relied more and more, had correctly predicted the reaction of ruling circles in Britain.

Potentially more disturbing than protests from Geneva and Stresa was the *rapprochement* between France and Russia. France had failed in 1934 to create an eastern Locarno to contain the Nazis. But Barthou's successor, Pierre Laval, had more success with Russia; on 2 May 1935 France and Russia concluded a formal alliance pledging mutual assistance against unprovoked aggression. Fourteen days later Russia concluded a pact with Czechoslovakia promising aid against aggression on condition that France honoured her pledges first.

The threat of a new encirclement failed to materialize, not least because of French mistrust of Russia. Germany's diplomatic position improved steadily throughout 1935 with a notable success in June with the signature of the Anglo-German naval convention. Misconceived though Hitler's analysis of British foreign policy undoubtedly was, a *rapprochement* with Britain was his aim from the mid-1920s onwards. In *Mein Kampf* he maintained that an understanding between the greatest continental power and the greatest sea power was the essential precondition of eastward expansion – a characteristic oversimplification completely ignoring Britain's continued interest in the European balance of power. Early in February 1933 Hitler told Admiral Raeder, commander-in-chief of the navy, that he would willingly acknowledge Britain's right to possess a large fleet commensurate with her world markets. In November 1934 he invited Britain – without success – to conclude a treaty on this basis. Immediately after the re-introduction of conscription when Sir John Simon and Anthony Eden, then Lord Privy Seal, visited Berlin in March 1935 Hitler again raised the subject. As the German foreign office seriously doubted whether Britain would be interested, the Führer appointed Ribbentrop, one of several unofficial 'experts' on foreign affairs, as his special emissary to further the project. This time the German offer was taken up in London. On 18 June a naval convention was signed which limited German tonnage to 35 per cent of that of Britain and her Commonwealth.

Hitler was highly delighted with Ribbentrop's success which represented a considerable diplomatic triumph for the Nazis. But at no cost to Germany. Naval expansion still went ahead as rapidly as possible after 1935. Clearly it would take some time before Germany reached the 35 per cent ceiling: firstly, because army and airforce would continue to enjoy priority for the foreseeable future and, secondly, because ship-building capacity was limited. That being so, Hitler saw no reason why he should not get political mileage out of the situation. Undoubtedly the naval convention, taken in conjunction with Hitler's careful avoidance of colonial questions, represented a calculated bid to win Britain over and free Germany for war against France and Russia in that order. Even so, Germany was already looking ahead to the day when the fleet might conceivably be used against Britain, i.e. in the second stage of German expansion. In June 1934 discussing the details of a major building programme Hitler and Raeder agreed that the fleet would have to be built up for use against Britain one day. So the naval convention changed nothing; indeed plans for the construction of super battleships virtually coincided with the signature of the agreement.

This is an appropriate point at which to refer to the part played by the so-called colonial question in Hitler's overall strategy. Way back in 1919 Hitler, like other nationalist agitators, demanded the return of Germany's former colonies. After 1924 and the decisive commitment to living space in the east he argued against colonial acquisitions, both on strategic grounds and because of the need for British friendship at least until such time as Germany dominated the continent.

As the Nazi party grew in the 1930s it incorporated in its ranks many old-style colonial enthusiasts particularly members of the Colonial Society which enjoyed support from shipping magnates, merchants and from some manufacturers. Hitler kept a tight rein on their propaganda up to the end of 1935 for the sake of the British alliance. When he stated publicly in March 1936 and again in September that Germany could not after all forgo her colonies, though economic factors were mentioned, his real hope was that this would force Britain to come to heel, much as William II's Germany blackmailed Britain over colonial issues in the 1890s.

Only at the end of 1937 does Hitler seem to have finally concluded that his attempts to secure a British alliance had failed, and that because of her hostility towards Germany war was inevitable sooner or later. The strategy outlined in *Mein Kampf* was thrown out of joint by this turn of events. For if war with Britain did come in his lifetime, Germany would be able to attain world status in the foreseeable future with the colonies which normally accompanied that status. However, as Hitler was preoccupied with Central Europe in 1938, he allowed the colonial campaign launched in 1937 to subside. So much so that on 3 March 1938 he assured Sir Nevile Henderson, the British ambassador in Berlin, that the colonial question could wait 'four, six or ten years' which probably meant (though the ambassador did not realize it) that Hitler envisaged a clash with Britain in the mid-1940s by which time Germany would be the dominant power in Europe.

Britain's failure to consult France and Italy in advance about the naval convention with Germany gravely weakened the Stresa Front. In the autumn it collapsed completely when Britain and France imposed sanctions on Italy following her attack on Abyssinia. During the African war which dragged on throughout the winter of 1935-6 Germany remained officially neutral, and imposed an embargo on exports of oil, textiles, fats, iron and steel – but not coal of which Italy had become the main buyer. Neutrality did not signify indifference to the outcome of the war. On the contrary; Hitler was keenly aware then, as later, that a long-drawn out conflict in Africa involving the Mediterranean powers would allow Germany freedom of manœuvre in Europe. Understandably, news of the Hoare–Laval Plan greatly upset the Germans; war had divided the Great Powers; peace would unite them and retard the realization of Hitler's ambitions. One authority remarks with some justification that Hitler was saved by British public opinion.[2] For the rejection of the plan destroyed all hopes of compromise. The war continued, Germany's diplomatic position grew stronger and as a bonus mark Italy drifted inevitably closer to Berlin, eventually bringing into being a new political combination: the Rome–Berlin Axis.

The close of 1936 saw Germany committed to far-reaching plans aimed ostensibly at economic self-sufficiency but in fact designed to prepare the nation for war in the not-too-distant future. To this aspect of the situation we must now turn.

Autarky or self-sufficiency was always a very popular concept in the Nazi party. The rank and file were taught to regard economics as part and parcel of the nation's struggle for existence. The *Völkischer Beobachter* depicted Germany as a beleaguered land ringed around by hostile powers and obliged to keep herself in a state of readiness for all emergencies. To simple-minded party

[2] E. Wiskemann, *The Rome Berlin Axis* (London, 1949), p. 52.

members – many with vivid memories of the hardships of the First World War – it seemed axiomatic that the less Germany bought abroad and the more she produced at home the better for German pride and security in wartime whether it made economic sense or not. The reluctance of many industrialists to cut themselves off from world markets made them suspect figures in a party which, in theory at any rate, was perfectly prepared to turn industry upside down to achieve its ends. Autarky as an economic objective corresponded with the radical and vaguely socialist mood of the party's lower echelons, an attitude shared by influential figures such as Goebbels and Bormann. Autarky was also Hitler's ideal. But in his case it meant much more than the exclusion of foreign imports. Autarky for him was the essential economic counterpart to the racialist dream of living space. In 1942, speaking of the advantages which would flow from the conquest of Russia, he declared that: 'We shall become the most self-supporting state in every respect including cotton in the world . . . timber we shall have in abundance, iron in limitless quantity, the greatest manganese-ore mines in the world, oil – we shall swim in it! And to handle it all, the whole strength of the entire German manpower.'[3]

In practice progress towards autarky in the generally accepted sense of producing as much as possible at home was painfully slow. In complete contrast to agriculture, on which the Nazis clamped a straitjacket of rigid controls in 1933, there was relatively little interference in industry. It does not follow that Hitler was well-disposed towards industry; in fact the memorandum from German industry and trade in 1933 advocating a liberal commercial policy to stimulate exports and also a reduction in government investment left him completely unimpressed. But he had no desire to offend influential industrialists whose co-operation was needed for speedy rearmament. Fortunately the existence of considerable unused capacity virtually excluded any direct conflict of interest between the demands of the war machine and the need for a general economic revival. For the time being Hitler could rely on industry to co-operate voluntarily with him. Accordingly, party interference in industry was forbidden in April 1933. A month later Hitler assured representatives of industry and banking that private enterprise would be the sheet-anchor of the

[3] H. Trevor-Roper, *Hitler's Table Talk, 1941–44* (London, 1953), p. 624.

Nazi economy, stressed that public works were a necessary evil to facilitate rearmament and promised tax reliefs for industry. Schacht's presence at the ministry of economics was an additional guarantee of industrial independence for he enjoyed a high reputation as an intrepid champion of free enterprise. In these circumstances Hitler left the question of whether industry should employ substitutes in place of foreign imports to the industrialists themselves.

Pressure for autarky came from several quarters outside the party. Heavy industry was the leading exponent of self-sufficiency from the earliest days with the giant chemical combine I.G. Farben leading the field. Ever since the First World War I.G. Farben had been interested in the production of synthetic fuel from coal by hydrogenation. In the early 1920s this appeared to be commercially viable as it was believed that world petroleum supplies would soon be exhausted. However, in the late 1920s new sources of supply were discovered. Shortly afterwards the Depression forced petrol prices down and completely jeopardized I. G. Farben's carefully-laid plans. The government refused to bail the firm out; the most Bruening would do was increase duties on foreign petroleum. These increases were bitterly assailed by the Nazis because they retarded the growth of the motor industry. As the odds against Hitler's accession to power shortened, I.G. Farben representatives met the Führer in the autumn of 1932, and persuaded him to stop the press campaign against high duties. There is no direct evidence that Hitler agreed to support I.G. Farben's autarkical schemes in return for financial aid, even though the firm contributed handsomely to party funds in February 1933.

Indeed, Hitler was at first attracted by the rival scheme of Gottfried Feder, the party's economic expert, for the construction of large refineries to process imported crude oil. In May 1933 Hitler actually approved the scheme largely because it would lead to the creation of new jobs in heavy engineering at a time when work creation had a high priority. That was not the end of the matter, for the oil producers raised serious financial and strategic objections; an increase in crude oil prices could easily wipe out any saving in foreign exchange; furthermore, refineries dependent on American supplies would obviously be vulnerable to blockade in wartime. In the second half of 1933 informed opinion moved in favour of hydrogenation. The growing influence of I.G. Farben was apparent in September when Carl Krauch, director of the Oppau works, secured army and airforce support for a four-year plan for the production of synthetic fuel. Nothing came of this initiative. But in December the government finally decided for I.G. Farben and concluded the so-called Feder–Bosch agreement with that firm. The autarky lobby had scored its first victory. Under the agreement prices and markets for petrol produced by hydrogenation at the Leuna works were guaranteed for ten years; in return I.G. Farben agreed to increase annual production to between 300 and 350,000 tons by December 1935.

Schacht's attitude to autarky was equivocal. He accepted the Feder–Bosch agreement and in 1934 actually compelled reluctant brown coal producers, who much preferred their own less efficient synthetic fuel process, to finance out of their own resources the construction of three hydrogenation works, all of which were completed by 1939. Such measures undoubtedly enabled Germany to meet the demand for light fuels out of her own resources as early as 1937. But Schacht was never an unrestrained advocate of autarky. It is perhaps significant that his ministry allowed the brown coal producers to drag their feet for several months until the army protested at the delay. All along Schacht had strong reservations about autarky appreciating that it would make a return to world markets more difficult after the completion of rearmament. On principle he refused to provide capital on a large scale for the production of raw materials at grossly uneconomic prices. He resisted constant pressure from the *Sonderaufgabe Deutsche Roh-und Werkstoffe*, an office set up by Hitler in 1934 independently of the ministry of economics for the specific purpose of ensuring that foreign raw materials were replaced by indigenous products wherever possible. When Wilhelm Keppler, head of this agency, appealed to Hitler to overrule Schacht, the Führer ordered him to avoid conflict with the minister having no desire to prejudice economic expansion at this stage for the sake of autarky.

Autarky also had strong support in the air ministry which was desperately anxious to secure reliable fuel supplies for the growing airforce. For broader strategic reasons autarky was favoured by the military economics and ordnance group (*Wehrwirtschafts und Waffenwesen*), a branch of the armed forces office (*Wehrmachtamt*),

set up in 1934 under Colonel Georg Thomas. Thomas believed
firmly in defence in depth, i.e. in the creation of an adequate
economic base for war, a fairly unpopular doctrine in military
circles which were mostly content to increase the size of the armed
forces. In the winter of 1933–4 Thomas, then head of the army
ordnance office (*Heereswaffenamt*), drafted a five-year plan to
co-ordinate the procurement of supplies by the armed forces and
to provide for the expansion of indigenous food and raw material
supplies. Thomas's campaign for autarky undoubtedly made
military circles more aware of the need for economic mobilization.
Like Keppler, Thomas encountered formidable obstacles. Plans
drawn up by I.G. Farben and the war ministry in December 1933
for the production of artificial rubber (*buna*) were vetoed by
Schacht on grounds of cost. When Blomberg returned to the
attack in June 1935 with a demand for general expansion of fuel
oil production, Schacht flatly refused. His fear was that such a
measure would upset the peacetime balance of the economy, and
he was still influential enough to postpone the issue until the
middle of 1936.

By this time Germany faced serious economic difficulties and
Schacht's influence had dwindled away. Despite his skilful hand-
ling of the situation, little room for manœuvre remained by 1936.
When Hitler insisted that the army reach its current target of
thirty-six divisions by the autumn, the additional burden proved
too great for a precariously balanced economy.

Several factors contributed to the general crisis which gripped
Germany in the second half of 1936. Firstly, the terms of trade
were worsening. Between 1929 and 1932 imports declined more
in price than exports. After 1933 the position was reversed with
imports either remaining stable or even increasing in price. But
the price of exports continued to fall though more slowly than
before. Broadly speaking import prices rose by 9 per cent between
1933 and 1936 while export prices fell by 9 per cent. This meant
that, compared with 1933, Germany had to export about 20
per cent more in 1936 in order to import the same quantity of
food and raw materials.

Secondly, German agriculture was increasingly unable to
satisfy the demands made of it. Aiming at autarky in agriculture
from the start, the Nazis set up the *Reichsnährstand*, an elaborate
organization which supervised all aspects of rural life from

production to distribution. Walter Darré, the minister of agriculture, succeeded in cutting food imports substantially. But
production declined steadily, partly because of poor harvests and
partly because of the ministry of agriculture's faulty pricing policy.
As consumer demand was increasing with the economic revival,
difficulties were unavoidable. Schacht strove to keep food imports
to a bare minimum to ease the strain on foreign exchange, but
came under increasing pressure to modify his position. In April
1935 he reluctantly authorized additional oilseed imports and in
October had to find 3 million *RM* for extra butter imports.
Friction between Schacht and Darré continued throughout the
summer of 1935. In the autumn Schacht bluntly refused to
provide foreign exchange for increased food imports in the hope
that he might force Hitler to face economic realities. This caused
the so-called 'bread crisis' when ministry officials seriously discussed the introduction of ration cards. Probably for the first time
Hitler was seriously worried by an economic problem, for he was
far too astute a politician not to realize how damaging rationing
might be to civilian morale. To resolve the difficulty whilst
avoiding a clash between Schacht and Darré, the Führer
appointed Goering as arbiter with orders to guarantee food
supplies. The dispute was resolved in Darré's favour with an
allocation of 12·4 million *RM* in December 1935. In February
1936 Darré requested 59·2 million *RM* for oil seed, twice the sum
spent in 1935. Schacht refused and again he was forced by Hitler
to find the necessary foreign exchange.

As the economic situation deteriorated, Germany found it
increasingly difficult to obtain the raw materials needed for
rearmament on the scale demanded by Hitler. World trade
reached a nadir in 1935; exports for 1935/6 fell below the 1933
level precisely when demand for food and raw material imports
was growing. In December 1935 Schacht told Blomberg that he
could not provide foreign exchange to pay for a doubling of
copper and lead imports as requested by the armed forces; furthermore, foreign exchange and raw materials for rearmament even
at the present level could not be guaranteed beyond April 1936.

By the end of 1935 Hitler was rapidly losing faith in Schacht,
for he sensed that the latter's quasi-liberal policies were now
totally inadequate to satisfy his own vaulting ambitions. For the
first time the Führer began to think seriously of taking positive

steps to encourage the production of indigenous raw materials, a matter previously left to private industry. In May 1935 he referred to the need for the use of synthetics in a Reichstag speech, and at the party rally in September he called for efforts to increase home production of specific raw materials: petrol, rubber and artificial fibres.[4] The imposition of sanctions on Fascist Italy in October following her attack on Abyssinia was an additional source of concern. It was not obvious then that sanctions would prove a broken reed. Had they succeeded Germany's enemies would have had an efficacious weapon at their disposal for bringing Hitler to heel as well.

Meanwhile the economic situation grew steadily worse. In March 1936 a serious fuel crisis was precipitated by a Russian embargo on exports to Germany and a Roumanian demand for higher prices or cash down for their oil exports. As the Germans resisted Roumanian pressure, supplies ceased abruptly and overnight half Germany's fuel was endangered. By this time Schacht's star was waning rapidly. Hitler in a desperate bid to solve the deepening crisis gave Goering overall control of raw materials and foreign exchange. In the months that followed Goering accumulated immense economic power in his own hands, power which he placed unhesitatingly at Hitler's disposal.

The economy had at last reached the crossroads. Drastic action was called for to avoid a major crisis. When the raw materials committee met on 26 May at Goering's request, an official stated that existing raw material stocks would last two months at most. Wool supplies would last two weeks, heating oil five weeks, diesel oil six weeks, light oil nine weeks and lubricating oils nine months. Home production could not possibly replace these imports. In the case of diesel oil, a vitally important ingredient of the modern war machine, only 9·5 per cent of requirements came from indigenous supplies and no improvement was likely in the near future. Nor was a sudden increase in exports the answer, as Schacht pointed out; a 25 per cent increase would be needed but 10 per cent was the most one could expect.

---

[4] D. Eichholtz, *Geschichte der deutschen Kriegswirtschaft, 1939–1945* (Berlin, 1969), I, pp. 40–41 suggests that a meeting between Goering and Krauch immediately prior to the rally may have influenced Hitler. It is significant, too, that after the rally Hitler told party leaders that he needed four years to be ready for war according to a ministry of the interior official. *VFZ*, 9, 1961, p. 28.

The pressure on the balance of payments continued to mount in the summer of 1936. In the second half of the year the ministry of agriculture's foreign exchange requirements amounted to 852 million *RM*, practically double the 1934 estimate. In August the war ministry demanded a 3,600 million *RM* increase in the military budget to bring the peacetime strength of the army up to thirty-six divisions by October and to complete the expansion of the airforce by the spring of 1937; to fulfil these tasks the armed forces asked for double the amount of raw materials used in 1935. Not surprisingly a financial crisis occurred in the summer. Germany faced a 500 million *RM* deficit and the munitions industry was obliged to work at 70 per cent of capacity through lack of raw materials. Goering's answer was the seizure of foreign stock held by German citizens and an acceleration in the payment of foreign debts, temporary measures strongly opposed by Schacht. That these steps, which produced 500 million *RM*, were nothing more than a desperate expedient was as clear to Goering as to the minister of economics.

To establish the facts, Goering asked several experts to submit memoranda on various aspects of the economic situation. One of the weightiest came from Carl Goerdeler, later one of the leading figures in the German resistance movement. Goerdeler's report, presented at the end of August, firmly rejected the trend to autarky and called for a return to free trade. To get the economy on to an even keel again, Goerdeler advocated cuts in raw material imports even at the risk of an unemployment level of two millions, a proposal which may well have reflected the views of powerful sections of German industry. Throughout the summer Hitler was kept fully informed of the economic situation. In August he discussed it with Goering probably on more than one occasion. So concerned was Hitler by official pressure for a curtailment of rearmament in the interests of economic stability, that in the end he put pen to paper, a rare event in itself, and produced an important memorandum which removes all doubt about his ultimate intentions.[5] One copy was given to Goering, another to Blomberg and in 1944 Albert Speer, then minister of armaments, received a third copy from Hitler himself.

In a lengthy preamble Hitler set the tone of the memorandum by declaring that conflict between Russia and Western Europe

[5] *DGFP*, C, V, no. 490.

was inevitable. Of all the western states only Germany (and Italy) were capable of repulsing the 'Jewish-bolshevik' threat, a rapidly-growing menace since Russia's introduction of conscription on 11 August 1936.[6] Whenever the historic confrontation occurred – and Hitler refused to commit himself to a date – one thing was certain; it would not end in another Versailles treaty but in the annihilation and destruction of the German people. In the face of this appalling danger all other considerations paled into insignificance. Rearmament could never be too great or too rapid. The message of the hour was crystal clear: 'If we do not succeed in developing the German Wehrmacht within the shortest possible time into the finest army in the world . . . Germany will be lost. The principle applies here that the omissions of peacetime months cannot be made good in centuries.'

As usual Hitler exaggerated the danger of conflict largely for internal propaganda purposes. Since 1935 the propaganda machine had pursued a strongly anti-Russian line. The Franco-Soviet and Soviet-Czech pacts were denounced as part of an encirclement plot; at the party rally in September 1935 Rosenberg delivered a vehement attack on 'Jewish bolshevism' to justify the new racial laws; and in 1936 the outbreak of civil war in Spain and the election of a Popular Front government in France were eagerly pounced on by the Nazi press as fresh evidence of the growing bolshevik menace. Of course, up to a point Hitler believed his own propaganda. At the same time, faced with mounting opposition to further increases in armaments from civil servants and economic experts, he played up the bolshevik bogy confident that this would stifle critical voices. It would also help to persuade the people that an extension of military service to two years was unavoidable. Anti-bolshevism had a deeper psychological significance. It supplied an external foe to bind the people closer to their leaders; it made it easier to brand critics of the regime as enemies of the state much as the Stalinists equated failure to fulfil the Five Year Plan with treason; and it is perhaps not too fanciful to suggest that by imputing aggressive designs to Russia the Nazis were preparing the nation for the war which was inevitable one day if Germany wanted living space.

[6] On 24 August Hitler increased the period of compulsory service to two years. Cf. François-Poncet's perceptive comments *DDF*, 2, III, nos. 198, 204, 209.

Territorial expansion, whatever the economic cost, was still
Hitler's aim as the brief economic analysis after the preamble
made plain. Overpopulation and rising living standards placed
an intolerable strain on Germany's food supplies – so the argument ran – and immediate action was imperative. Almost as a
matter of course Hitler remarked that the long-term answer was
the acquisition of living space; 'it is the task of the political
leadership', he went on, 'one day to solve this problem.'

That lay in the future. For the present Germany had to make
do within the limits of existing resources. Hitler made it absolutely
clear that he would permit no retardation of rearmament. From
this decision everything else followed. Additional foreign exchange
would not be made available to pay for increased food imports.
Nor could extra foreign exchange be earned abroad at a time of
intense foreign competition in world markets – not that Hitler
was remotely interested in closer ties with the outside world.
How, then, could Germany break out of the deepening crisis
created by his own stubborn insistence on accelerating the pace of
rearmament? Hitler's answer in one word was autarky. Germany
must produce more of the raw materials she needed at home *as far
as possible*. The qualification was important; it cannot be emphasized too strongly that Hitler understood perfectly well the impossibility of attaining complete self-sufficiency within Germany's
existing frontiers. Even so, autarky would make Germany less
dependent on foreign sources of supply and would save foreign
exchange badly needed for essential food imports in peacetime.
Therefore Hitler called for increases in the production of synthetic rubber, iron-ore, fats, textiles and light metals, in fact 100
per cent self-sufficiency wherever possible. With the recent fuel
crisis very much in mind he insisted on a solution of the fuel
problem within eighteen months – an utterly impossible demand
which seems to have originated in a draft scheme prepared by
Krauch and his I.G. Farben associates and shown to Hitler by
Goering. The Führer further insisted that the fuel problem be
tackled with the same determination 'as the waging of war; for on
its solution depends the conduct of the future war', another
unmistakable sign of Hitler's intentions.

When Hitler handed Speer the memorandum in 1944 he
recalled that it was written in order to combat 'the lack of understanding of the ministry of economics and the opposition of

German business to all far-reaching plans'. The experts' tiresome habit of harping on production costs infuriated Hitler. Was it not better, he wrote indignantly, to produce dearer tyres from indigenous material rather than talk of making them out of cheaper foreign rubber which Germany could not in fact afford to buy? Similarly, he brushed aside as totally irrelevant opposition from the ministry to the use of indigenous iron-ore because its low ferrous content would double or treble costs. Most revealingly, he opposed bitterly suggestions for stockpiling raw materials at the expense of current production of arms and munitions (the policy of General Thomas); 'it would nonetheless be better for the nation to enter the war without one kilogram of stocks of copper but with full munitions depots, rather than with empty depots but so-called "enriched" stocks of raw materials.' He doubted whether a state could stockpile for a war lasting more than one year. But even if this were possible, leaders who preferred to stock-pile copper and iron instead of making grenades ought to be hanged in his opinion. For the war he had in mind – this is a point of crucial importance – would have to be a short swift campaign. From the beginning he appreciated all too clearly that Germany lacked the resources to wage a major war.[7]

Objections from private industry did not move him. The honeymoon with the industrialists ended in 1936. If the private sector could not face up to the demands of autarky, he threatened to resort to state intervention to attain his ends: 'it will not be Germany who will go under but at most, a few industrialists'. Economics, on the surface at any rate, still played a subordinate role in his scheme of things: 'finance and economics and all theories are there to serve the struggle of a people to assert itself'. Will power was the answer to every problem. How an economic mobilization 'comparable to the military and political mobiliza-tion' was achieved was of no concern to him as long as there was no interference with the pace of rearmament. What mattered was the objective which he stated with unmistakable clarity at the end of the memorandum: 'the German army must be operational

[7] Cf. Hitler's comment to Brauchitsch and Halder 27 September 1939: 'In general, time will work against us if we don't exploit it to the utmost. Economic resources on the other side stronger; (opponents) are in a position to purchase and to transport.' F. Halder, *Kriegstagebuch* (Stuttgart, 1962), I, p. 86; cf. *NCA*, VIII, L–52, p. 801.

within four years' and 'the German economy must be fit for war
within four years'.

For tactical reasons Hitler made no reference to living space
when introducing the Four Year Plan at the party rally on 9
September.[8] To judge by his speech autarky was simply intended
to save foreign exchange and keep men in employment when the
rearmament programme was completed.. Hitler's appeal to the
people to support the plan fell on ready ears because the depression had shattered the belief in *laissez faire* economics and made
peoples everywhere look more and more to the state for economic
salvation. Schacht, despite his genuine commitment to liberal
trading policies, helped to smooth the way for autarky by demon-
strating how effective state intervention could be in excluding
unwanted imports. Under the New Plan imports fell from 9 per
cent in 1933 to 7 per cent in 1935; the corollary was a decline in
exports from 10·5 per cent of the national income in 1933 to
7·2 per cent in 1935. Autarky did not of course automatically
commit Germany to war. It is arguable that even had rearmament been cut, Germany would still have had to produce more at
home to save precious foreign exchange and so reduce her
dependence on the outside world when markets for her exports
were increasingly difficult to obtain. It was Hitler's decisive
intervention in the economic field in the summer of 1936 which
ensured that autarky would not be employed to protect living
standards in Germany but simply to serve the Nazis' imperialist
ambitions. The primary purpose of the Four Year Plan was to be
the preparation of Germany for war, hence the high priority given
to the production of fuel oil and rubber from the start.

The choice of Goering to supervise the Plan was further proof
of Hitler's determination to have his own way. Goering, a verit-
able mayor of the palace now at the height of his power, was
regarded as the party's strong man who would brook no opposition to the Führer's will. Quite correctly the French ambassador
observed that the appointment of Goering and his first decree on
the Four Year Plan on 22 October represented 'a new chapter in

[8] But addressing the Labour Front on 12 September Hitler hinted unmistakably at his ultimate objective: 'If we had at our disposal the incalculable
wealth and raw material of the Ural mountains and the unending fertile plains
of the Ukraine to be exploited under National Socialist leadership, then we
would produce and our German people would swim in plenty. . . .' N. Baynes,
op. cit., I, p. 929; cf. *DDF*, 2, III, no. 250.

the history of the Third Reich'.[9] What amounted almost to a Hitler–Goering axis came into being to prepare Germany for war.

Goering left no doubt in the minds of his associates about Hitler's objectives. Addressing the council of ministers on 4 September with a copy of Hitler's memorandum in his hand, Goering declared that war with Russia was inevitable: 'all the measures have to follow as if we were already in a state of imminent mobilization'.[10] In December, speaking to his airforce commanders, he went even further: 'the conflict which we are moving towards demands a gigantic degree of productivity. The end of rearmament is not in sight. The only decisive factor here is victory or defeat. When we win, the economy will be sufficiently compensated. One cannot apply simple book-keeping principles of profit in the situation but only the needs of the political situation. One mustn't calculate what it costs . . . we are playing for the highest stakes . . . we are already in a state of mobilization and at war, the only difference is that there is no shooting yet.'[11]

While there is no doubt about Hitler and Goering's determination to prepare the economy for military adventures, we must not be misled by Goering's sanguine outbursts into imagining that the Four Year Plan signified the total mobilization of the Germany economy for war. Recent research has revealed that, like so much in the Third Reich, the reality fell far short of the claims of the propaganda machine. Planning in Nazi Germany was only partial in the late 1930s, in no way comparable to the Russian experience. As long as the Nazis relied on private enterprise – which they continued to do in the main despite Hitler's dire threats to industrialists – large-scale planning embracing the entire economic life of the people was impossible. Considerable sectors of the economy, such as consumer goods, remained outside the scope of the plan. Up to the summer of 1938 the plan covered a fairly wide range of economic activity not directly related to war preparations. Only at the height of the war after Stalingrad did pressure for total mobilization become irresistible. Hitler postponed drastic action in the economic sphere as long as possible for several reasons. He was too astute a politician not to appreciate

[9] *DDF*, 2, III, no. 417, p. 643.
[10] *IMT*, XXXVI, 416–EC, p. 491.
[11] W. Treue, 'Das dritte Reich und die Westmächte auf dem Balkan', *VFZ*, I, 1953, *FN*, pp. 53–4; cf. *NCA*, VI, 3474–PS.

that the concentration of economic power in a few hands – the inevitable consequence of total mobilization – would be a potential threat to his own supremacy. It would also arouse opposition within the party especially from the *Gauleiter* who behaved like feudal barons in their own districts and exerted some control over local industry. And, most weighty objection of all, Hitler's plans did not call for re-structuring of the economy. All that was required was rapid expansion of the armed forces for short victorious campaigns with limited objectives. By 1936 it had become clear that raw material shortages would impede re-armament unless determined efforts were made to reduce dependence on the outside world in respect of fuel oil and rubber, hence the introduction of autarkical measures. But the Four Year Plan was almost in the nature of an adjunct to rearmament, an economic *Blitzkrieg* plan and not an attempt to switch from rearmament in breadth to rearmament in depth.

It is no part of this book to evaluate the impact of the Four Year Plan on the economy as a whole. But the internal political consequences of the Plan are of some interest. It has been argued that up to 1936 the interests of German industry more or less coincided with those of the party and the army.[12] This fragile 'coalition', if that is not too strong a word for it, was shattered by the economic crisis of the summer. Schacht was horrified to learn of Hitler's plans on 2 September. It was his belief that autarky on the scale envisaged would antagonize foreign opinion and reduce German exports, a view widely shared in banking circles and by Ruhr industrialists. But when Schacht sought Blomberg's help in dissuading Hitler from his plans, the minister of war declined to co-operate. The generals had grown somewhat suspicious of Schacht, seeing in his attempts to control the military budget evidence that he was lukewarm about rearmament. In any event, autarky seemed to offer a more secure base for rearmament free from the vagaries of international trade.

Nor did Schacht have the whole of industry on his side. Industries such as chemicals, aluminium, aircraft and synthetic textiles were less interested in external markets and stood to gain from subsidized production for the home market. Therefore they welcomed the Four Year Plan. It is no coincidence that the

[12] A. Schweitzer, *Big Business in the Third Reich* (London, 1964), especially Chapter II; but D. Eichholtz, *op. cit.*, pp. 48–50.

influence of I.G. Farben was increasing rapidly in 1936. When Goering became commissioner for raw materials in April 1936 he immediately claimed jurisdiction over synthetics and recruited Carl Krauch to his staff. Krauch played a leading role in drafting the Four Year Plan in conjunction with the economic division of the war ministry. Not surprisingly 45 per cent of the total investment under the plan between October 1936 and July 1938 was in synthetic products and chemicals. In effect, a powerful coalition of party officials, leading generals in the war ministry and I.G. Farben directors had come into being with a vested interest in military expansion at all costs.

For twelve months Schacht fought a losing battle against the autarky lobby. His worst fears were soon realized. In April 1937 he protested vigorously to Goering about Germany's failure to increase exports when world trade was reviving at long last. The ever-increasing arms burden and the demands of the Four Year Plan were to blame for this in Schacht's opinion. Increased demand for raw materials had pushed up domestic prices, a further disincentive for exporters who were already experiencing extreme difficulty in obtaining raw materials. Far from saving raw materials, Goering's Plan had simply exacerbated the position in the short run. Schacht insisted that cuts in rearmament and in the Four Year Plan were essential to permit a renewed export drive. Needless to say, Hitler and Goering brushed that advice aside. Only because Schacht had an international reputation to which the Nazis attached importance, did Goering bother to appease him by calling a conference on exports in May.

The struggle between Schacht and Goering reached a climax over the use of low-grade ores. For strategic reasons Hitler was anxious to reduce German dependence on Swedish ores. Much to Goering's surprise he encountered opposition from the steel masters. They argued that the use of ores with a ferrous content of 30 per cent would be unprofitable and would adversely affect exports. It would also saddle them with spare capacity when the rearmament boom ended. Schacht shared these objections and actively encouraged the resistance. However, under heavy pressure from party and army, the steel masters finally agreed to co-operate but only on condition that steel prices were raised by 50 per cent. Rather than submit to blackmail, Goering carried out Hitler's threat to rely on state intervention where private industry failed the nation. In July 1937 a state-owned steel corporation, known later as the *Reichswerke Hermann Goering,* was founded. This bold stroke divided the opposition. Only six steel magnates were prepared to sign a protest against the confiscation of private ore deposits and in defence of the inalienable right of private industry to provide additional steel capacity. The remainder, after a stern warning from Goering to the effect that further resistance would be regarded as sabotage, decided that discretion was the better part of valour.

Goering had won a decisive victory over industrial opposition to his plans. Schacht was more anxious than ever to resign. In the late summer of 1937 he confronted Hitler at Berchtesgaden. The Führer swept out of a stormy interview complaining to Speer that Schacht was upsetting his plans. For reasons of general policy Hitler hesitated to dispense with Schacht's services even when the latter ceased to appear at work in the hope of forcing the Führer to act. Only when it was patently obvious that he had no alternative, did Hitler accept Schacht's resignation on 26 November 1937. The primacy of Goering in economic matters was complete. It is not without some interest that exactly three weeks before this, on 5 November at the Hossbach conference, Hitler spelt out the military implications of the new economic policy.

At the close of 1937, as Schacht withdrew from active politics, the shadow of a serious economic crisis was already looming on the horizon. Basically, the Nazis were facing the problems consequent upon the overheating of an economy. The mounting arms burden, investment in the Four Year Plan together with a lavish building programme – which for prestige reasons the Nazis refused to abandon even after the outbreak of the war – strained the economy beyond its capacity once full employment was virtually achieved by December 1936.

The first sign of trouble was the appearance of an acute labour shortage in the building, building-materials and metal industries, all closely associated with rearmament. The consequences were serious. Army orders could not be met on time. Pressure on wages and prices increased until the controls, on which the Nazis had relied since 1933 to check consumer demand, started to burst at the seams. Wage increases were conceded in key industries. Even strikes were 'no longer an exceptional occurrence' according to a ministry report in August 1936. Piracy of scarce labour resources by industrial rivals became widespread. Even in sectors un-affected by these symptoms discontent was caused by the spectacle of affluence elsewhere. A decline in the quantity and quality of consumer goods intensified the upward movement of wages and prices and added to the general feeling of malaise in the working class. Finally, the decline in exports, caused by a loss of skilled workers to the booming contract industries, further exacerbated the competition for scarce raw materials.

The Nazi leadership was perturbed and perplexed by these problems. Though the Nazis employed draconian measures to stifle political opposition, they hesitated to grasp the economic nettle firmly. Curiously enough, in some respects dictatorships seem more responsive to public feeling than other forms of government. From *Gestapo* reports Goering was keenly aware of the unresolved tension lying beneath the surface conformity of the masses, and was therefore reluctant to impose rigid controls on the working class in an attempt to delay the inevitable econ-omic explosion.

Hitler was as well informed as anyone in government circles of the general economic situation, though whether he bothered to read in full regular reports from the ministry of labour we cannot know for certain, and on the whole it is unlikely. From the docu-mentary evidence available it is impossible to establish any casual relationship between Hitler's awareness of the deepening crisis and the gathering pace of German foreign policy after November 1937. Nor should one expect to find evidence of this sort. Ideological, strategic and economic factors are too closely intermeshed in a country's foreign policy to permit of a clinical separation. The inter-relationship appears only as part of the total historical process, not in isolation from it. What one can say in the case of Nazi Germany is that the politico-strategic assumptions on which Hitler operated and the consequential priorities he imposed on the economy created stresses and strains which in turn confirmed him in the correctness of his original diagnosis and strengthened him in the belief that time was running out for Germany.

CHAPTER FOUR

From the Rhineland Re-Occupation to the Hossbach Memorandum

THE re-occupation of the Rhineland in March 1936 was a real turning-point in the interwar years. This was not just because Hitler scored a great diplomatic victory at the expense of Britain and France and at no cost to himself. In military terms he had closed the open flank in the west so that when the time came for Germany to move eastwards she would have no need to fear French reprisals. It is no accident that, as the military balance started to tip towards Germany, Hitler began to adopt a more aggressive stance in international affairs. Generally speaking, before 1936 he had relied on the negative reactions of the major powers to advance towards his goal. After the re-occupation of the Rhineland, however, he relied increasingly on violence, or the threat of violence, to attain his objectives.

Originally, Hitler did not intend to seize the Rhineland before the spring of 1937. But evidence of British military weakness, the deepening internal crisis in France, Russia's desire for peace and the fact that Italy, bogged down in Abyssinia, desired a *rapprochement* with Germany created especially favourable conditions for a forward policy in 1936. Domestic considerations may well have played some part in Hitler's decision. Certainly Neurath thought that Hitler, worried about declining enthusiasm for the regime, hoped to whip up popular support by a foreign success. Hassell, the German ambassador in Italy, agreed that internal affairs were uppermost in Hitler's mind but added the revealing comment that the Führer was consumed by an 'irresistible itch for action' in which he was actively encouraged by the sycophantic Ribbentrop. That seems to be borne out by Hitler's comment on 19 February that as Italy and Germany were surrounded by democracies 'tainted by bolshevism', 'passivity was in the long run no policy . . . attack in this case too was the better strategy'.[1] As a pretext for action Hitler pounced on the news that the Franco–Soviet Pact was soon to be ratified; this, so he argued, was incompatible with the Locarno Pacts and would automatically release Germany from the obligations entered into freely in 1925 in respect of the demilitarization of the Rhineland.

With characteristic caution he moved towards the objective. Although he told Fritsch on 12 February that he intended to re-occupy the Rhineland, in fact he did not feel free to move until 3 March when Mussolini assured him that Italy would not support counter measures against Germany. On 4 March the foreign affairs committee of the French Senate approved the Franco-Soviet alliance. The next day Hitler ordered Blomberg to move troops into the Rhineland within forty-eight hours. On 7 March infantry battalions marched into Trier, Aachen and Saarbrücken to be greeted enthusiastically by the local populace. The military operation was accompanied by the usual 'peace offensive' at which Hitler was rapidly becoming a past-master.

First reactions were encouraging. Britain deplored the breach of treaty but did not see in Hitler's action a threat to peace. France decided that military resistance would be futile. But on 8 March Premier Sarraut declared in a spirited radio broadcast that France would never negotiate as long as Strasbourg was menaced by German guns. An alarmed Hitler murmured re-assuringly about his pacific intentions.[2] Two days later Flandin, the French foreign minister, persuaded Britain to take a more serious view of the re-occupation. When the German military attaché sent alarming reports to Berlin on 12–13 March of the warlike situation in London, a worried Blomberg urged withdrawal on Hitler. It used to be thought that the latter was bluffing and would have ordered an immediate withdrawal without a shot being fired had the French marched in. We now know that this was not the case.[3] Military directives issued by Blomberg and Fritsch early in March envisaged a fighting withdrawal in the

[1] E. M. Robertson (ed.), 'Zur Wiederbesetzung des Rheinlandes', *VFZ*, 10, 1962, p. 192.

[2] He told Schmidt that the forty-eight hours after the re-occupation were the most nerve-racking in his life: P. Schmidt, *Statist auf diplomatischer Bühne, 1923–1945* (Frankfurt, 1949), p. 320; cf. K. von Schuschnigg, *Ein Requiem Rot-Weiss-Rot* (Zürich, 1946), p. 43.

[3] D. C. Watt, 'German plans for the re-occupation of the Rhineland: a note', *JCH*, 1966.

face of superior forces. Of course, Hitler did not believe that France would intervene. The important point, however, is his willingness to risk hostilities even in 1936 rather than lose face. Confronted by Blomberg, Hitler was critical of his minister's 'weak nerves'. The armed forces office did not share Blomberg's fears. Nor did Neurath who advised Hitler to await official reactions abroad before countermanding his orders.

Sound advice. Britain, in deference to public opinion and Commonwealth sensibilities, was not prepared to coerce Hitler. In the end the matter was referred to the League. That body merely condemned Germany's action and proposed that the International Court adjudicate on the compatibility of the Franco–Russian alliance with the Locarno Pacts; until such time as the court reported Germany should refrain from constructing fortifications in the Rhineland. As Germany virtually ignored the suggestion, nothing came of it.

The collapse of the Stresa Front had other important consequences for Germany. On 11 July an important agreement restored normal relations with Austria. Out of deference to Mussolini, Germany had to promise not to interfere in the internal affairs of Austria. Nevertheless, the agreement taken as a whole greatly strengthened Germany's position. Schuschnigg, the Austrian chancellor, was acutely conscious of the growing power of Austria's neighbour, and prepared to pay a heavy price to prevent Italy and Germany reaching agreement at Austria's expense. He conceded that Austrian foreign policy must be co-ordinated with Germany's; he promised to release several thousand Nazis and to allow German newspapers in Austria again; and he even agreed to give the so-called 'national opposition' seats in the cabinet. It was, as an American observer remarked, 'the first critical step in the disintegration and eventual downfall of Austria'.[4] Hitler at once summoned the Austrian Nazi leaders to the Berghof and ordered them to respect the new agreement. Of course, while Schuschnigg regarded it as the maximum concession possible to preserve Austrian independence, Hitler saw in it only a halfway house on the road to complete assimilation – but only when circumstances were favourable, which they

[4] *NCA*, V, 2385–PS, p. 37. Hitler's initial reactions were adverse until favourable public reactions convinced him of his error; F. von Papen, *op. cit.*, pp. 370–2.

were not as long as Mussolini was still interested in the fate of Austria.

Six days later the Spanish Civil War broke out. The origins of German involvement are of some interest. On the whole party organizations exerted no decisive influence on German policy despite much huffing and puffing. Spain was the exception. When civil war broke out, the German foreign office adopted an attitude of strict neutrality. That did not satisfy the *Auslandsorganisation*, another Nazi party agency meddling in foreign affairs. One of their agents in Spain, Johannes Bernhardt, saw economic possibilities in the sale of war material to the rebels. Accompanied by a colleague he flew to Berlin carrying letters from Franco requesting war material. The foreign office refused to receive them. Whereupon they contacted Gauleiter Bohle, head of the *AO*. Through Hess he arranged for them to meet Hitler at Bayreuth. Fresh from a session of Wagnerian opera and without consulting Neurath or Ribbentrop, Hitler agreed to help Franco. Some circumstantial evidence suggests that Goering's interest in Spanish raw materials may have played an important part in Hitler's decision.[5] Other factors were certainly involved. No doubt on ideological grounds he was easily convinced that fascist powers must exorcise the spectre of 'Red' Spain. And he must also have appreciated that Franco's victory would give the French another front to defend in time of war.

The German commitment in Spain was limited and never equalled Italy's in terms of men and materials. All the same, for a relatively modest outlay Goering obtained access to valuable raw material supplies at a time when Britain was competing seriously for Swedish ores. By 1937 1,600,000 tons of iron-ore and 956,000 tons of pyrites had been shipped to Germany without any expenditure of foreign exchange. And once the prospect of a swift victory for Franco receded, the strategic advantages of the war became apparent. A 100 per cent victory for Franco was undesirable, as Hitler commented at the Hossbach conference: 'we are more interested in the continuation of the war and the preservation of tensions in the Mediterranean' he remarked on that occasion; for this would exacerbate the political divisions in France and might divert the western powers' attention from Eastern Europe to the Mediterranean area.

[5] G. Weinberg, *op. cit.*, pp. 289–90.

The Spanish Civil War had another advantage for Hitler. It tied Italy down in the Iberian peninsula, thus removing the only remaining obstacle to a forward policy in Eastern and South-eastern Europe. By September 1936 Hitler was ready for a *rapprochement* with Italy. Mussolini was equally anxious to come to terms once he realized that the Civil War would be a long struggle. In October Count Ciano, the Italian foreign minister, visited Germany and protocols were signed covering a variety of topics from the recognition of Manchukuo to the creation of an anti-bolshevik front. The latter theme was developed with gusto by Hitler during Ciano's visit to the Berghof. What Hitler had in mind was a powerful front able to stand up to the western powers. Faced with this formidable combination, he believed that Britain might well come to terms with the dictators. Hitler was now less sure of a British alliance than in 1935 for he went on to say that if Britain continued to thwart them, they would be able to defeat her. Germany would be ready for war in three years, 'in four years more than ready, if five years are given, better still' – an estimate corresponding to his comments in the August memorandum.[6] The October protocols remained unpublished but on 1 November in a speech at Milan Mussolini revealed the existence of a general agreement between the two countries, and spoke of an axis 'around which all those European states which are animated by a desire for collaboration and peace may work together'.

The German foreign office was perfectly well aware of the significance of the Rhineland re-occupation. In a remarkably frank conversation with the American ambassador Neurath admitted that until the Rhineland had been digested no active steps would be taken in foreign affairs. Everything possible would be done to prevent trouble in Austria and a conciliatory policy would be pursued towards Czechoslovakia. Once the western frontier had been fortified and the countries of Central Europe understood that France could not invade Germany at will, things would change: 'all those countries would begin to feel very differently about their foreign policies and a new constellation will develop'.[7]

---

[6] *Ciano's Diplomatic Papers* (London, 1948), p. 58.
[7] *NCA*, VII, L–150.

Neurath's prognosis proved remarkably accurate. On 5 November 1937 Hitler summoned his commanders-in-chief to the Chancellery and in the presence of Neurath and Blomberg harangued them at length on the need for a more dynamic foreign policy. A summary of the proceedings exists in the so-called Hossbach Memorandum drawn up by Hitler's adjutant a few days later.[8] The accuracy of the account has been questioned but there is no compelling reason to doubt that, broadly speaking, the memorandum is a reasonably accurate summary of Hitler's remarks.

What did Hitler say on that dark November afternoon? He commenced with a solemn declaration that this was to be his political testament, the product of his cogitations over the last four and a half years. At the outset he stated in uncompromising terms his belief that the aim of German policy was to preserve the racial community and to enlarge it. Territorial expansion would not only preserve Germanism outside the *Reich*; it would also provide the food needed to sustain eighty-five million Germans. As was customary on these occasions, Hitler paraded the well-worn economic arguments to 'prove' his contention. Was autarky the answer to Germany's pressing economic difficulties, he asked? Even in 1936 he had never pretended that. Germany was, he admitted, self-sufficient in respect of coal, iron and light metals but not even in copper and tin – ergo, complete autarky was not possible in respect of raw materials. It was even more certain that autarky could not solve the food problem. For one thing, soil deteriorated under intensive cultivation. And even when home production did increase, any surplus was swallowed up in rising living standards. The admission that living standards could not be lowered is a significant one. Ostensibly this was because Europe had a common living standard; in fact, he recognized only too clearly the limits of his own power. Continuing, he asked whether Germany could solve her food problem by increasing her share of world markets? That was impossible, Hitler argued; Germany just did not have sufficient foreign exchange to import all the food she needed especially when harvests failed; furthermore, as food-producing areas became industrialized they would have less food to export. No, the fact was that mankind lived in an age of economic empires. Japan and Italy were compelled to

[8] *DGFP*, D, I, no. 19.

expand by economic necessity 'and with Germany too economic need would supply the stimulus', he declared. Strategy was important, too. As long as Britain controlled the world's sea-lanes, a Germany dependent on world markets was vulnerable to attack in wartime. One solution only remained: Germany must acquire new space for agricultural use and for sources of raw materials. That this entailed the use of force was crystal clear: 'Germany's problems could only be solved by means of force and this was never without attendant risk.' The issue was simply when and how Germany could 'achieve the greatest gain at the lowest cost.'

As usual, Hitler introduced a note of urgency into the picture. After 1943/5 he predicted a deterioration in Germany's position. The advantage her army possessed at present over other countries would diminish as equipment became obsolete and her opponents rearmed. Secondly, in view of the scarcity of foreign exchange, a new food crisis could occur any year. 'One thing only was certain': Germany could not wait longer than 1943/5 at the latest to solve her problems. With his gift for oversimplification he summed up the position succinctly: 'On the one hand there was the great *Wehrmacht* and the necessity of maintaining it at its present level, the ageing of the movement and of its leaders; and on the other, the prospect of a lowering of the standard of living and of a limitation of the birth rate which left no choice but to act.' So he arrived at the nub of the problem: whatever the economic cost, he stubbornly refused to contemplate even a temporary reduction in the pace of rearmament. At the same time his sensitive political antennae informed him that if he attempted to ride out the inevitable economic crisis by deliberately depressing living standards, the basis of the dictatorship would be undermined. Logically, that left expansion as the only way out of a self-imposed dilemma.

There followed a long and rambling disquisition about the possibility of expansion before 1943/5. Hitler dilated on the possibility of civil war in France or of war between Britain, France and Italy which he alleged was likely in the summer of 1938. In either event Germany would seize Czechoslovakia 'with lightning speed'. These territorial acquisitions would greatly strengthen Germany's frontiers and release forces for other purposes, an observation which made it abundantly apparent that his aim was the expansion of Germany, not the defence of German minorities. Throughout the speech Hitler was at pains to reassure the commanders-in-chief that general war could be avoided because the western powers had probably written off Czechoslovakia and would not, therefore, intervene.

Such was the Hossbach Memorandum. When a version of it came into American hands in 1945 it was used to substantiate count three of the indictment against the major war criminals at Nuremberg, i.e. that they planned and waged aggressive wars. During the trial the British prosecuting counsel spoke of 'the plot . . . divulged at the Hossbach meeting'.[9] In his closing address the American attorney commented that 'as early as November 5 1937 the plan to attack had begun to take definiteness as to time and victim'.[10] And in their findings the Tribunal itself agreed that the seizure of Austria and Czechoslovakia was both 'premeditated' and 'carefully planned'.

That was a quarter of a century ago immediately after the collapse of the Third Reich when contemporaries readily assumed that Nazi aggression from the Rhineland re-occupation to the attack on Russia had been a cleverly-planned operation. Today no historian would subscribe to that view. Some, notably Alan Taylor, have denied that the Hossbach conference had any significance at all.[11] The case is a strong one. We know that Hitler called the meeting because of the smouldering dispute between Blomberg and Goering over raw materials allocations to the armed forces. Blomberg bitterly resented the way in which Goering abused his position as plenipotentiary for the Four Year Plan to favour the airforce, and urged Hitler to take some action. Characteristically, Hitler refused to take sides, having no wish to offend Goering, his right-hand man. In the end the Führer called a special conference at which he may have hoped to divert attention from the quarrel by talking about foreign policy, a field where he was undisputed master. Another important factor was Hitler's desire to accelerate the pace of rearmament; as he told Goering, he hoped to stampede the cautious Fritsch into a more co-operative frame of mind and had Neurath in attendance simply to impress the generals. Hitler undoubtedly exaggerated the

[9] *NCA* Supplement A, p. 81.
[10] *NCA* Supplement A, p. 20.
[11] A. Taylor, *op. cit.*, pp. 131–4.

danger of war to impress his audience.[12] It is significant that he
spoke of the 'seizure' of Austria in complete contradiction to the
evolutionary policy he was now following. Goering commented
justifiably that Hitler had often spoken in general terms about his
'plans', so there was no good reason to attach special importance
to this meeting as the prosecution had done; Hitler always tailored
speeches to suit his audience and would very likely have employed
different arguments to convince a conference of diplomats. If one
looks dispassionately at the memorandum, nothing remotely
resembling a 'plan' is discernible. Nor is it proper to use the word
'plot', as a collective decision did not emerge from the meeting.
In the discussion following Hitler's speech on 5 November Blomberg and Fritsch expressed alarm at the prospect of offensive
warfare in the near future. When Fritsch spoke of postponing his
annual leave, Hitler hastily conceded that the matter was not
urgent – an admission which might be seen as proof that he had
been exaggerating all along. Finally, if one accepts Taylor's
interpretation, another puzzle is solved; when Hossbach submitted his (unsolicited) memorandum to Hitler for his approval,
the Führer twice refused to read his 'political testament', conduct
which suggests that he had lost interest in the meeting after it had
served its immediate purpose.

While there is much in this interpretation which cannot be
gainsaid, it is not the whole truth. Hitler spoke more openly on
5 November of his intention to use force in the pursuit of his
objectives than ever before. Of those present at the meeting
Fritsch, Neurath and Hossbach were all alarmed by these dangerous undertones though Blomberg shrugged it off, as so often
before, and the simple-minded Raeder readily accepted Goering's
bland assurance that it was all an elaborate charade.

The commitment to violence was no passing aberration. When
Hitler's remarks are seen – as they should be – in the context of
his speeches in the winter of 1937/8, a significant pattern emerges.
On 21 November, addressing party officials at Augsburg, Hitler
spoke of the 'new tasks' facing Germany on account of her inadequate *Lebensraum*. At present the world evaded the issue. One
day it would have to understand the problem. The most difficult
part of the Nazis' preparatory work was over. The party and the

[12] Ribbentrop testified to Hitler's conviction that soldiers had always to be
addressed as if war was imminent; *IMT*, X, p. 359.

people must now close its ranks behind the leader so that 'relying on the strength of a people of sixty-eight millions expressed in the last resort by its army', he could accomplish 'the tasks which are set before us'.[13] Two days later at Sonthofen Hitler spoke to political cadets about the urgent need for adequate living space if Germany was to survive and of the need to create tough tenacious leaders ruthless in upholding the national interest. 'Then a state in arms will arise . . . a "state in arms" not only because everyone will bear arms from the young to the old but because they are spiritually armed and ready to use the arms if need be.'[14] Again, on 22 January 1938 Hitler emphasized the difficulty of the food situation in an address to senior generals, and insisted that Germany would have to obtain new space by force. These arguments were repeated on 28 May during the first Czech crisis. One can only conclude that Hitler's attitude hardened quite suddenly in the late autumn of 1937, and that he made up his mind to pursue a more adventurous policy at the risk of war if need be.

To what combination of factors can we attribute this change of attitude? Without doubt military considerations were of paramount importance. The whole purpose of rearmament was to put Germany in a position of maximum strength relative to her opponents as quickly as possible. The danger was that once these opponents grew apprehensive and commenced to rearm, Germany's military advantage would rapidly disappear, certainly by 1943/5. Obsolescence of weapons was another constant reminder that time was not on Hitler's side. Go forward he might; stand still he dare not because that meant falling behind. Or as he put it on 5 November: 'It was while the rest of the world was still preparing its defences that we were obliged to take the offensive.'

Secondly, the international situation favoured a dynamic foreign policy. Since the formation of the Axis the balance of power had swung rapidly towards Berlin. Italy was not lured back into the Anglo-French camp after Abyssinia but remained the firm friend of Germany. The Duce's state visit in September 1937 cemented the friendship and gave Mussolini an opportunity to tell Hitler of his irritation with Schuschnigg's policy. Hitler also noted with satisfaction how Italy was sinking deeper in the mire

[13] N. Baynes, *op. cit.*, II, p. 1370.
[14] H. Picker, *Hitlers Tischgespräche im Führerhauptquartier, 1941–42* (Bonn, 1951), p. 450.

of the civil war in Spain, leaving Germany free to move forward in the east.

In the west France was gravely weakened by the collapse of the Locarno system in 1936. For although Britain offered a guarantee to France in November 1936, Eden, now foreign secretary, made it abundantly clear that this did not extend to her eastern allies. To complicate matters still further, Belgium lapsed into neutrality again. At the same time the Nazis' anti-bolshevik campaign was having some effect on western statesmen who inclined to see in Nazi Germany a bulwark against communism, a point which emerged clearly during Lord Halifax's visit in November 1937. Finally, the weakness of Soviet Russia was dramatically illustrated by the purges in the summer of 1937 which decimated the top echelons of the Red army.

Disillusionment with Britain probably had some bearing on Hitler's decision to move forward more quickly. He had hoped that Ribbentrop, appointed ambassador to Britain in August 1936, might swing her on to Germany's side. Had he succeeded, France would have been completely isolated and Germany would have become master of Europe overnight. During 1937 the vision faded. Despite – or perhaps because of – Ribbentrop's blandishments Britain evinced no interest in the Anti-Comintern Pact signed by Germany and Japan in November 1936. Mistrust of Germany was on the increase and by the summer of 1937 British rearmament was gathering pace. When Ribbentrop visited Mussolini in October 1937 he admitted that the London mission had failed and added that the interests of Britain and Germany were irreconcilable. On 6 November 1937 Ciano signed the Anti-Comintern Pact; Axis and Pact were at last amalgamated and an anti-bolshevik triumvirate came into being. When Hitler referred to Britain and France as 'hate-inspired antagonists' at the Hossbach meeting, it was clear that he had now largely abandoned hopes of an English alliance. Though he still hoped that Britain, because of her military weakness, would be unable to interfere in Europe, nevertheless he accepted the premise that Germany would have to reckon with general British opposition to eastward expansion; that made it all the more urgent to accelerate the tempo of his policy.

Fourthly, Hitler was becoming increasingly preoccupied with his own mortality at the close of 1937. In October he informed his propaganda chiefs that he had not much longer to live and must, therefore, solve the living space problem as quickly as possible; future generations could not do this, only he could. According to Albert Speer, Hitler complained of stomach disorders towards the end of 1937 and expressed anxiety about deteriorating health.[15] Addressing senior generals on 22 January 1938 he again spoke of shattered nerves and sleepless nights. These morbid thoughts probably strengthened his conviction that he 'could wait no longer' as he told Neurath when the latter tried to dissuade him from war.

Finally, economic and social factors played their part in Hitler's decision. The living space arguments advanced on 5 November were not in themselves proof of this because they were clearly irrelevant to the problems of an overheated economy where shortage of labour, not shortage of land, was the major difficulty. On the other hand Hitler was aware that the Nazi movement was losing its 'demonic edge'. In an opaque passage on 5 November he spoke of the impossibility of arresting the decline of Germanism in Austria and Czechoslovakia and even in Germany itself. Sterility was setting in and 'disorders of a social nature' would arise in time. The problem referred to was a real one though it was socio-economic in origin, not racial as Hitler imagined. With the attainment of full employment the social and economic aspirations of the people were growing, and what interest they had in foreign adventures was waning. Being heavily committed to rearmament, the Nazis could not satisfy these aspirations. Therefore, in the last resort the only way of maintaining a façade of unity at home and preventing the gradual erosion of the dictatorship would be the pursuit of an active foreign policy, i.e. the acquisition of living space in the east. What Hitler realized, however vaguely and imperfectly, in the winter of 1937/8 was, as a historian of the period has observed, that 'the Third Reich had either to set itself new tasks by expanding or . . . cease from being totalitarian'.[16]

To sum up: at the end of 1937 Hitler felt that great gains could be made at low cost out of the unfolding situation. For that reason he wanted to accelerate the pace of rearmament, in itself

---

[15] A. Speer, *Erinnerungen* (Frankfurt a.M.–Berlin, 1969), p. 120.

[16] T. W. Mason, 'Some origins of the Second World War', *Past and Present*, 29, 1964, p. 69; cf. N. Baynes, *op. cit.*, II, p. 1273.

surely proof of aggressive intent. There was no 'plot' or 'conspiracy', but the Nuremberg prosecution team was perfectly correct in maintaining that 'the Hossbach memorandum removes any possible doubt about the Nazis' premeditation of their crimes against peace' provided that we substitute Hitler for 'Nazis'. Or, as a recent writer put it aptly: even if this was not a timetable for aggression, it was a ticket for the journey.[17] Hitler was relying on his instincts on 5 November. How he would move forward he did not know, only that he intended to do so in the not-too-distant future. Nothing happened immediately after the Hossbach meeting for the obvious reason that forward action depended on favourable opportunities arising, such as war in the Mediterranean. It is unwise to assume from Hitler's inaction that he had merely been talking for effect to divert attention from internal disputes, though this may well have been a secondary consideration.

It is in the military sphere that we find conclusive proof of a decisive change in Hitler's policy in the winter of 1937/8. Blomberg informed Keitel, head of the armed forces office, of the Hossbach conference, and he in turn informed Jodl, head of operations in the high command. Jodl then learnt that Goering had already ordered changes in the airforce directive to reflect the new policy. Fearing that unilateral action by the airforce would undermine the position of the high command *vis-à-vis* the three commands, Jodl obtained Blomberg's permission to draft an amendment to the general directive of June 1937.[18]

Up to this point German strategic planning – carried out, incidentally, without reference to Hitler – had been essentially defensive in character. Ever since the drastic reduction of Germany's armed forces in 1919 she had been vulnerable to attack from her neighbours France, Poland and Czechoslovakia, either separately or in coalition. The Non-Aggression Pact of 1934 temporarily removed the very real fear of attack from Poland. Late in 1935 the general staff drew up their first major deployment plan, *Plan Red*, to ward off a major French attack on the assumption that France's ally, Czechoslovakia, while assisting

---

[17] G. Brook-Shepherd, *Anschluss* (London, 1963), pp. 11–12.

[18] *NCA*, VI, 175–C. This, the second annual directive to be issued, was intended to co-ordinate the work of the three branches of the armed forces. The contents of the first directive in June 1936 are unknown.

the French, would not play an offensive role. However, the possibility of a Czech offensive at a crucial moment in the struggle in the west could not be entirely discounted, especially after the Franco–Soviet Pact opened up the prospect of Russian air power operating from Czech bases. In May 1935, after staff discussions in the armed forces office, Blomberg issued instructions for *Schulung*, a military exercise to prepare a detailed study on the feasibility of a surprise attack on Czechoslovakia. Beck, chief of the general staff, denounced *Schulung* as a military absurdity certain to lead to war with Britain as well as France, and flatly refused to implement the order. No doubt professional jealousy between army command and Blomberg's armed forces office had much to do with Beck's flagrant disobedience. By 1937 Beck was finally persuaded to agree to the preparation of an alternative deployment plan, *Plan Green*, for a pre-emptive strike at Czechoslovakia to forestall offensive action by that power during a war in the west. It was Schlieffen in reverse; a lightning strike at Czechoslovakia before switching the army westwards for the decisive battles against France. In the directive of June 1937, which formalized the strategic planning to date, *Plan Green* took second place to *Red*, and because of Beck's sceptical attitude little work was done on it in practice. Meinck is probably right up to a point in interpreting *Plan Green* as a purely routine exercise based on the probability of joint military action by France, Czechoslovakia and Russia.[19] Taken on its own, *Plan Green* is not proof that Blomberg was planning aggressive warfare. But some passages in the preamble certainly suggest that Blomberg drafted the directive with guidance from Hitler. For having discounted the possibility of aggressive warfare by other powers, Blomberg remarked disingenuously that the German army must be ready, if called upon, to exploit 'favourable political opportunities' and spoke of war in 1937/8 as a possibility, remarks which have an unmistakably aggressive flavour about them. It is just conceivable that the politically-naïve Blomberg did not fully appreciate the aggressive implications of this language.

Whilst there can be legitimate differences of opinion about Blomberg's directive, there is little doubt that Jodl's amendment

[19] G. Meinck, *op. cit.*, pp. 127–41; cf. O'Neill, *op. cit.*, p. 123. For a different interpretation E. M. Robertson, *Hitler's Pre-war Policy and Military Plans, 1933–39* (London, 1963), p. 92.

of 7 December 1937 removes all ambiguity from the picture.[20] It represented a decisive shift of emphasis in strategic planning. 'When Germany has achieved complete preparedness for war in all fields', he wrote, 'the military conditions will have been created for carrying out an offensive war against Czechoslovakia so that the solution of the German problem of living space can be carried to a victorious end even if one or other of the Great Powers intervene against us', i.e. when Germany was fully prepared for war she would attack Czechoslovakia, not to remove a threat to Germany's rear as in the past, but to prepare the way for a successful *Drang nach Osten*. At the same time Jodl emphasized that Germany must not be trapped in a two-front war, so that if the situation was unfavourable *Plan Green* might be postponed for several years. However, if France and Italy were at war in the near future and if Britain remained neutral leaving only Russia to come to the help of the Czechs, then Germany would attack Czechoslovakia regardless of the fact that she was not fully prepared for war. What did it all mean? In the first place, *Plan Green* now took precedence over *Plan Red* in all planning. Secondly, Germany was now committed to the pre-emptive strike against Czechoslovakia in time of peace. Thirdly, the object of war was no longer the defence of the *Reich* against a hostile coalition of powers, but rather the conquest of foreign territory, i.e. Bohemia and Moravia plus an *Anschluss* with Austria. On 13 December Hitler signed Blomberg's supplementary directive and on 21 December copies were sent to the three service chiefs. As a result of the initiative taken by representatives of the armed forces high command, *Plan Green* was transformed from a defensive strategy into the keystone of an offensive plan inspired by Hitler and designed to serve the ends of National Socialist imperialism.

[20] *DGFP*, D, VII, pp. 635–7. One may disregard Jodl's submission at Nuremberg that there was nothing sensational in what he learnt of the Hossbach conference and that only minor corrections of existing directives were necessary; *IMT*, XV, p. 456.

CHAPTER FIVE

Gathering pace: Austria and Czechoslovakia, 1938

On 12 January 1938 Field-Marshal von Blomberg married his secretary, Erna Gruhn, at a civil ceremony attended by Hitler and Goering. Twelve days later Goering informed Hitler that Blomberg's wife was a prostitute well-known to the Berlin police. At the same time he produced documents which purported to prove that Fritsch had been guilty of homosexual practices. This allegation was so ludicrous to anyone who knew the stiff old-fashioned soldier that even Hitler, when shown the 'evidence' in 1936, peremptorily ordered its destruction. It is impossible to say whether he was genuinely shocked by the renewal of the allegations. Undoubtedly there was a strong Puritanical streak in his character and he was always prepared to believe the worst of the officer corps.

It has been suggested that the opposition expressed by Blomberg and Fritsch to Hitler's plans on 5 November 1937 was the direct cause of their dismissal.[1] No doubt, as Hitler listened silently to the sharp exchanges between Blomberg, Fritsch and Goering, he must have been disturbed by their defeatist attitude. But there is no proof of any direct connection between the two soldiers' opposition on 5 November and their removal from office in January 1938. Indeed, in Blomberg's case Hitler had every reason to be well satisfied with the minister of war's performance. In April 1938 Hitler openly expressed his indebtedness to Blomberg for the successful integration of the conservative-minded officer corps in the National Socialist state. Again, in September 1939, he remarked that he would never forget the services rendered

[1] P. Graf von Kielmannsegg, 'Die militärpolitische Tragweite der Hossbachbesprechung' in *VFZ*, 8, 1960. For a different interpretation H. Gackenholz, 'Reichskanzlei, 5 November 1937' in *Forschungen zu Staat und Verfassung. Festgabe für Fritz Hartung* (Berlin, 1958).

by Blomberg in ridding the army of many reactionary officers.

Fritsch was a different proposition. If Blomberg had to go because his *mésalliance* violated the strict code of conduct of the officer corps as well as arousing Hitler's personal displeasure, the natural successor would be Fritsch. Under no circumstances was Hitler willing to have this cautious conservative as commander-in-chief of the armed forces in view of his continual opposition to overhasty rearmament. So without further reflection he decided to use the charges against Fritsch to force the latter out of office. On 25 January Blomberg was told to resign, which he did meekly enough, being assured by Hitler that he would be recalled 'when Germany's hour struck' (which he never was). The following evening Hitler demanded Fritsch's resignation.

On Goering's recommendation General von Brauchitsch, a somewhat weak-willed and easy-going character, was appointed commander-in-chief of the army on 3 February after promising Hitler that he would bring the army closer to the state. Blomberg was not replaced. In the end, on Blomberg's own suggestion, Hitler assumed personal command of the armed forces on 4 February. The war ministry was abolished. Out of the old armed forces office Hitler created a personal military staff, the armed forces high command (*Oberkommando der Wehrmacht*), presided over by Wilhelm Keitel. Keitel, another compliant character completely under the Führer's spell, exercised the authority of the former minister of war and was given a status equivalent to that of other ministers.[2]

Possibly because he feared a hostile reaction from the officer corps, Hitler presented the structural changes as part of a wider reorganization. The sycophantic Ribbentrop was appointed foreign minister in place of Neurath (whose opposition to Hitler's plans had been a minor source of irritation), and at last the foreign office became a completely subservient tool of the Führer's. The ambassadors in Rome, Vienna and Tokyo were recalled. Fourteen generals hostile to the Nazis were compulsorily retired and forty-six reassigned. When the announcement was made public on 4 February, Hitler called senior generals together to explain his reasons for removing Blomberg and Fritsch, as well as to reassure

[2] On being told that by Blomberg that Keitel was only the man who ran the office, Hitler exclaimed: 'That's exactly the man I am looking for': W. Warlimont, *Inside Hitler's Headquarters* (London, 1964), p. 615.

them that the centralization of command in his hands was not an attack on the armed forces as such.

These dramatic changes shifted the balance of power very firmly in Hitler's direction. Quite possibly he welcomed a foreign political diversion at this juncture to divert attention from a potentially dangerous internal situation. The occasion arose on 5 February when Papen arrived from Vienna bewildered by his own recall which had upset delicate negotiations on the very eve of success. In January the Viennese police unearthed an Austrian Nazi plot to foment disorders and Austro–German relations deteriorated sharply. Schuschnigg, worried that Hitler might be reverting to the radical methods of 1934, expressed a wish to meet the Führer in the near future. Papen found Hitler preoccupied with the internal crisis. On hearing Papen's news he brightened up: 'That is an excellent idea,' he exclaimed. 'Please go to Vienna immediately and arrange for us to meet within the next few days.'[3]

The meeting between Hitler and Schuschnigg at the Berghof on 12 February was another diplomatic triumph for the Führer as well as being a classic example of the technique of intimidation practised by a master of the craft. At the outset Schuschnigg was bullied unmercifully by an irate Hitler who threatened to clear up the Austrian question once and for all but gave the Austrian chancellor 'one last chance' to see reason. Ribbentrop and Papen presented Schuschnigg with demands ranging from an amnesty for Austrian Nazis to the inclusion of the crypto-Nazi, Seyss-Inquart, in the cabinet, all of which they knew from their private intelligence Schuschnigg was willing to concede. Hitler had worked himself into a towering rage by this time and, summoning Schuschnigg to his study, insisted that the latter agree to the demands or take the consequences. When Schuschnigg protested, Hitler ushered him out and shouted for Keitel, a masterly stroke designed only to frighten the Austrian. Then another swift change of mood when Schuschnigg, having signed the memorandum, was given three days to secure his cabinet's consent. The final touch of genius was Hitler's order that rumours of mobilization be spread to unnerve the Austrians.

The elaborate charade was completely successful. The Austrian cabinet was sufficiently intimidated to accept the demands in their totality. Hitler was quite satisfied with the Berchtesgaden

---

[3] F. von Papen, *op. cit.*, p. 408.

agreement. It gave him all he had hoped for and he at once impressed upon the Austrian Nazis that 'he did not now desire a solution by violent means if it could at all be avoided'.[4] To make assurance doubly sure, Leopold, the radical-minded Austrian Nazi leader, was abruptly dismissed.

The invasion and annexation of Austria a month later was an unexpected development. When Schuschnigg resolved upon a desperate dash for freedom and announced on 9 March the holding of a plebiscite to enable the Austrians to determine their own future, he precipitated a crisis which forced Hitler's hand. Schuschnigg was 'responsible' for what happened only in the sense that a householder surprising an intruder at dead of night might be held 'responsible' for injuries received while trying to apprehend the burglar. The key to the situation was Hitler's fear that a positive vote for a 'free, German, independent, social Christian united Austria' would erect a formidable barrier to *Anschluss* at a later date. Because *Anschluss* was an essential preliminary to eastward expansion, Schuschnigg's initiative threatened to sabotage Hitler's whole programme.

It is unnecessary to recount the story of the next few days. What is interesting is the caution with which Hitler handled the situation. Beck and Manstein, his chief of operations, were summoned to the chancellery and ordered to prepare for invasion. The order led to frantic improvization; there was in fact no invasion plan, only *Plan Otto* to deal with the remote contingency of a Habsburg restoration and on that no work had been done because of Beck's opposition to the armed forces office. Yet even when Hitler signed the order on 10 March, he added an escape clause that he would only invade if 'other measures' failed, i.e. he preferred to undermine the citadel from within through the good offices of Seyss-Inquart, a leading Austrian Nazi now in Schuschnigg's cabinet. When news arrived of the cancellation of the plebiscite Hitler was easily persuaded by Goering – the leading protagonist of a violent solution – to exploit the advantage and oust Schuschnigg from power. Ribbentrop's confident assertion that Britain would not intervene played its part in the decision to force the pace of events.

Under pressure Schuschnigg resigned but President Miklas, in a last burst of defiance, refused to appoint Seyss-Inquart in his

[4] *DGFP*, D, I, no. 328.

place. Goering's vehement pleas for immediate invasion failed to convince Hitler. Warnings from Neurath and Papen and protests from London and Paris reminded him of the international ramifications of the Austrian problem while the absence of a reply from Mussolini to his urgent personal letter was disturbing. However, the turning-point on the evening of 11 March was the news of Schuschnigg's broadcast in which the chancellor announed that Austria yielded to force and ordered the army not to resist an invasion and so avoid the shedding of German blood. Hitler was immensely relieved. Had the German army been obliged to fight its way into Vienna, his reputation would have suffered irreparable harm, to say nothing of the near certainty of Great Power intervention. Coming out of the telephone booth with Goering chattering excitedly at his side, he resolved to act at once. The invasion was ordered for the next morning. With some difficulty Goering arranged a formal invitation from the crypto-Nazis on which Hitler insisted to preserve the semblance of legality. The final touch was added by a message from Hitler's envoy in Rome informing him that the Duce had declared his disinterestedness in Austria.

On 12 March the seventh and thirteenth corps together with the second Panzer division entered Austria. So hastily improvised was the entire operation that the tanks refuelled at petrol stations on the road to Vienna and the Panzer commander used a Baedeker guide to plan his route. Even now Hitler's caution did not desert him. Only after receiving a tumultuous reception in Linz did he abandon the idea of a satellite government under Seyss-Inquart and decide on annexation. On 13 March a subservient Austrian cabinet drafted a new law making Austria a province of the German *Reich*.

As a result of the *Anschluss* the balance of power in South-eastern Europe moved sharply in Germany's favour. Control of Vienna gave the Germans a dominant position in the Balkans. In the south Germany now possessed a common frontier with Italy while in the north Czechoslovakia's strategic position suddenly worsened; her defences were outflanked and her chances of survival diminished accordingly. Germany was strengthened, too, by the addition of 100,000 men to her armed forces comprising two infantry divisions, two mountain divisions and one light division.

The economic advantages of the *Anschluss* were far from negligible. Some additional steel capacity and ore mines, especially the Erzberger mines with their superior grade ore, fell into German hands, also Austria's foreign exchange reserves. In 1937 Germany only kept her payments in balance by raiding her reserves. Yet despite the accelerated tempo of rearmament and a growing demand for raw materials her luck still held out in the early months of 1938. One reason was a fall in import prices, sure sign of a fresh crisis later on. The other reason was the seizure of Austria's reserves amounting to 440 million *RM*. After allowing 145 million *RM* to cover Austrian requirements, the balance of 295 million *RM* wiped out the German deficit of 175 million *RM*, and left 140 million *RM* for raw material purchases. In this way the threat of a cut in raw material imports, apparently unavoidable at the beginning of 1938, was temporarily averted.

The conquest of Austria had been accomplished with much less difficulty than Hitler had ever imagined in November 1937. The western powers acquiesced in the *fait accompli*. Britain, though highly critical of Hitler's methods, felt that an *Anschluss* was inevitable and difficult to resist on moral grounds while France, deeply uncertain of herself, was only too relieved to use the British attitude as an alibi for her own inaction. Elated by the ease of the victory, Hitler immediately turned his attention to Czechoslovakia.

Hitler's lively hatred of the Czechs was a legacy of his pre-war days in Vienna where the Czech struggle for autonomy had alarmed German racialists anxious to preserve the German character of the Habsburg Empire against the 'advancing Slav hordes'. Post-war Czechoslovakia, a state with strong democratic traditions and forming an integral part of the Versailles system, was doubly obnoxious to Hitler. But basically military strategy determined his attitude to Czechoslovakia in 1938. Though he made great play with the 'threat' Czechoslovakia represented to Germany on account of its strategic position and its alliance with Russia, in fact the German army command was not particularly worried about either. The simple truth, as Bismarck once observed, was that control of Bohemia was the key to Eastern Europe. For that reason the destruction of Czechoslovakia was Hitler's objective from the outset.

The grievances of three and a half million Germans in the strategically-important Sudetenland were simply a convenient means to further Hitler's imperialist ambitions, nothing more. Nazi ideas spread rapidly in the Sudetenland after 1933 feeding on economic depression and local grievances. Early in 1938 Konrad Henlein, leader of the Nazi Sudeten German Party, rejected Czech offers of administrative decentralization and demanded autonomy for the Sudetenland inside the Czech state. So far Henlein had been an independent operator, in touch with Hess but with a fairly free hand to decide policy. In October 1937, after the Teplitz–Schönau incident when Nazi supporters clashed with Czech police, Henlein crossed the Rubicon. On 19 November he informed Hitler that the only satisfactory solution to Sudeten grievances was the incorporation of Bohemia, Moravia and Silesia in the Reich.[5] In effect Henlein placed his party at the Führer's disposal supplying the latter with a secret weapon for the disruption of Czechoslovakia.

The *Anschluss* made the spirits of the Sudeten Germans soar. There were rumours of invasion and excited talk of the 'return home to the *Reich*'. Hitler encouraged this mood. When Henlein visited him in March the Führer declared that he would solve the Sudeten problem in the 'not-too-distant future'. The Sudetens should demand so much that the Czechs would be unable to accommodate them but they must not drive things too far, because Hitler had no wish to precipitate a crisis before his plans were properly laid.

The international situation boded well for Hitler's scheme. All the indications were that Britain and France would remain passive. Italian goodwill had counted for something during the *Anschluss* crisis. Similarly, over Czechoslovakia Hitler relied on Italian involvement in the Mediterranean to give him a free hand. When the Anglo-Italian agreement was signed in April 1938 the German foreign office and the naval command congratulated themselves on having reduced the danger of a war in the Mediterranean certain to involve Germany. Hitler reacted differently. If Mussolini really believed that his Mediterranean mission was over, then Czechoslovakia must be postponed until

[5] In fact most of Henlein's followers wanted only autonomy inside Czechoslovakia; H. von Rimschka, 'Zur Gleichschaltung der deutschen Volksgruppen durch das dritte Reich', *HZ*, 1956, p. 60.

the distant future. But if Mussolini still believed in African expansion, 'Czechoslovakia (was) in the bag'.[6]

On 21 April Hitler, in his new role as commander-in-chief of the armed forces, discussed plans for the attack on Czechoslovakia with Keitel. Speed, they agreed, was absolutely essential for success. Victory must be assured within four days to prevent foreign intervention. France would hesitate to fight but Russia would 'very probably' aid the Czechs. Hitler attached great importance to correct political timing. Naked aggression he rejected, observing cynically that that technique could only be used against Germany's last continental foe. For the present world opinion had to be respected. Therefore Germany could attack Czechoslovakia either after a period of mounting tension, during which psychological warfare would weaken Czech resistance, or after a provocative incident, such as the murder of the German ambassador, which would put the Czechs in the wrong. On 20 May Keitel submitted a draft directive containing these points for the Führer's approval. Included in the text was Hitler's observation that he did not intend to 'smash Czechoslovakia without provocation in the near future through military action'.[7] Action would be taken only if internal developments in Czechoslovakia forced the issue or if an especially favourable international situation presented itself.

A week later Hitler's attitude changed dramatically. At a special conference of senior generals, foreign office and party officials on 28 May Hitler announced his 'unshakable will that Czechoslovakia shall be wiped off the map'.[8] Significantly, the attack on Czechoslovakia was depicted as part of a much broader strategy to acquire living space which Britain and France would certainly resist by force. When that moment arrived, Czechoslovakia would present a threat to Germany's rear. Therefore Czechoslovakia must be eliminated by a lightning stroke as soon as possible. At present serious opposition need not be feared. Britain and France did not want war, Russia would not intervene (a change of attitude here) and Italy was uninterested. He summed up the broad strategy thus: '. . . we will first tackle the situation in the east. Then I will give you three to four years time and then we will settle the situation in the west.'[9] Two days later

[6] *DGFP*, D, II, no. 132.			[7] *NCA*, III, 388–PS, p. 311.
[8] *NCA*, V, 3037–PS, p. 743.				[9] *Ibid.*, p. 744.

Hitler signed the final amended directive for *Plan Green* in which he stated bluntly that it was his 'unalterable decision to smash Czechoslovakia by military action in the near future'.[10] An accompanying letter from Keitel to the army commanders stated that the operation must be completed by 1 October at the latest.

Why did Hitler change his mind about the timing of the operation? Jodl believed the week-end crisis of 20/21 May to be the reason. False rumours of German troop movements stampeded the nervous Czechs into partial mobilization, whereupon Britain and France warned Germany against aggression and the crisis petered out. No doubt Hitler was infuriated by later reports that western opinion was convinced their governments' firm stand had at last checked the headstrong dictator. But it is possible that military considerations were equally important. During the week-end crisis Hitler was at the Berghof reviewing *Plan Green*. He appreciated that the *Anschluss* had given Germany a temporary advantage in Central Europe by outflanking Czechoslovakia's formidable fortifications. Now the clockwork precision of Czech mobilization made it clear how rapidly this asset was diminishing, hence the sooner the attack was launched the better.

Military planning went ahead with all speed with Hitler taking a close personal interest in the detailed preparations. On his express instructions formal mobilization was avoided because it would alert Germany's opponents and provoke counter measures certain to eliminate the element of surprise essential for swift victory. On the other hand, the necessary military build-up could not be completely disguised. The army hit on an ingenious solution; the war office announced the calling up of reservists on a limited scale from mid-August ostensibly to test mobilization arrangements and to give reservists routine training during the autumn manœuvres. Because of the 'routine' nature of the exercise, foreign powers found it difficult to lodge objections about the inflammatory political consequences of the German build-up. The very frankness of the war office misled some observers into thinking that it was all part of a cunning political campaign to intimidate the Czechs and make them amenable to a settlement. In reality it was a clever double bluff as others suspected. Whatever the war office pretended, it amounted to partial mobilization of the active army, as the British military attaché in Berlin

[10] *NCA*, III, 388–PS, p. 316.

observed. By the time the Munich Conference met partial mobilization had proceeded so far, in his opinion, that Germany could have launched an offensive immediately without waiting a further three days for full mobilization.[11] The German general staff was frankly amazed by the success of their stratagem. Even when the Czechs woke up to the danger by mid-September they still did not mobilize in retaliation. This was due partly to veiled threats from Germany but most of all to the restraining influence of Britain and France. As late as 23 September they were advising Czechoslovakia against mobilization pending the outcome of negotiations.

The Germans made strenuous efforts to disguise their military preparations. For example, some reservists were ostentatiously demobilized after training while the majority remained with the colours. The training, incidentally, was far from 'routine'; it included special exercises for an attack on the Czech fortifications. When the time came to move divisions into assault positions, great care was taken to travel by night and under camouflage, so important was the surprise element held to be.

Quite different tactics were adopted in the west where Hitler deliberately drew attention to the sudden acceleration of work on the West Wall. Incensed by reports that little progress had been made on these fortifications, Hitler loudly accused the generals of 'sabotage' and called in the Nazi work force, *Organisation Todt*, to speed up the work. In fact, Hitler knew perfectly well that Todt could not construct a line of viable defensive positions from Aachen to Basle in the five months between April and September 1938. His hope, as some contemporaries shrewdly surmised, was that signs of feverish and much-publicized activity would deter the French from an attack.[12]

On the whole the army co-operated loyally in the military preparations. Nevertheless, some opposition to Hitler's policy showed itself at a high level in the summer of 1938. The central figure was General Beck, now chief of the general staff. Alarmed by the tone of Hitler's pronouncements since November 1937, Beck submitted several memoranda to Brauchitsch, all highly critical on professional grounds of the projected attack on Czecho-

[11] *DBFP*, III, iii, appendix III, enclosure to no. 12.
[12] *DBFP*, III, i, no. 532; cf. E. Röhricht, *Pflicht und Gewissen* (Stuttgart, 1965), p. 127.

slovakia. One memorandum was discussed by senior officers at a secret meeting on 4 August convened by Brauchitsch himself. It is indicative of the attitude of senior officers towards Hitler that, whilst agreeing fully with Beck, they dispersed without pledging themselves to act. When Hitler saw the memorandum and learnt that Brauchitsch – showing spirit for once – had dared to read it to the assembled officers, he immediately summoned a meeting of army chiefs of staff and staff officers on 10 August at the Berghof. By calling younger officers together – an unorthodox step – he hoped to counteract the influence of the 'reactionary' senior men. In this he was disappointed. After Hitler's address General Wietersheim spoke of the weakness of the West Wall, quoting a remark of General Adam's, commander of the army in the west, that the wall could be held for three weeks at most. The angry Führer retorted that it 'could be held for not only three weeks but for three years: the man who does not hold these fortifications is a scoundrel'.[13] Opposition of any kind, even when the objection was a valid one as he must have realized on this occasion, simply strengthened his resolve to defy the facts. On 15 August senior generals were informed peremptorily at Jüterbog that he would solve the Czech question by force by 1 October; this time no discussion was allowed.

The political crisis in Czechoslovakia which had smouldered on throughout the summer suddenly deepened in September. When Benes, the Czech premier, agreed on 4 September to the Sudeten German demand for autonomy inside Czechoslovakia, their leaders were thrown into confusion. Henlein hastily seized upon a local incident at Moravska–Ostrava, where it was alleged the deputy leader of the party had been assaulted by a Czech policeman, to terminate the embarrassing negotiations with Benes. On 12 September in a violent address to the Nuremberg party rally Hitler ranted about the 'oppressed' Sudetens and demanded 'justice' for them, a masterly performance which raised the political temperature without committing Hitler to a time limit or even to territorial demands. Henlein did not miss the cue. His followers, carefully briefed in advance, staged uprisings on 13 September which failed ignominiously. Whereupon Henlein and his followers fled to Germany and from there issued a call to arms against the 'Hussite-bolshevik criminals of Prague'.

[13] *Jodl's Diary*, 10 August 1938.

The situation was shaping exactly as Hitler anticipated. Britain and France were doing everything possible, as the Runciman mission proved, to avoid war. Italy could be relied upon absolutely; on 15 September Ciano assured Germany that Italy would support her 'regardless of how the situation developed'. At home the harvest was in and military preparations were reaching a climax. On 3 September Hitler summoned Keitel and Brauchitsch to the Berghof for a final review of *Plan Green*. Dissatisfied with some of the details, he summoned them again on 9 September during the party rally for an exhaustive conference which lasted into the early hours. Finally, all was settled to Hitler's satisfaction.[14] The 'provocative incident', which the directive of 24 August specified as the pretext for armed intervention, would assuredly have occurred within a few days of the Nuremberg rally speech.

Suddenly the whole timetable was upset on 13 September when Chamberlain proposed top level discussions on the crisis. Hitler was taken by surprise, flattered perhaps that a British prime minister was flying out to meet him though it is difficult to believe that he expected Chamberlain to threaten armed intervention as he pretended later; British behaviour since May suggested that this was the last thought in Chamberlain's head.

Any doubt was quickly dispelled when Hitler met the prime minster at Berchtesgaden. Chamberlain's proposal for detaching the Sudetenland had little attraction for Hitler whose mind was set on the complete destruction of Czechoslovakia. Very likely Hitler thought he had seen the last of the 'umbrella politician' for it was inconceivable to him that Britain and France would meekly dismantle the Czech state. Clapping his hands with glee, he boasted to Ribbentrop and Weizsäcker that he had manœuvred 'the dry civilian' into a corner.[15] After Chamberlain's departure military preparations went ahead without interruption. On 18 September time schedules for the five invasion armies were approved and Hitler confirmed the selection of their commanders. To undermine Czech morale still further, the Germans

[14] The argument was about the use of armed formations. Hitler, thoroughly enjoying himself in the role of amateur stategist, insisted that the tanks, instead of being fragmented to support infantry attacks, should be concentrated for a break-through at the weakest point in the Czech defences with Prague as the objective.

[15] E. von Weizsäcker, *Memoirs* (Chicago, 1951), p. 150.

encouraged Slovak demands for autonomy. The same day, 20 September, Hitler berated the Hungarian premier and foreign secretary for failing to demand the return of Magyar minorities under Czech rule. On 22 September the Hungarians took the hint, after hearing that Poland was demanding the return of Teschen.

Meanwhile Chamberlain returned to Germany on 22 September. At the Bad Godesberg meeting with Hitler he formally offered to cede the Sudetenland without plebiscite. To his astonishment and dismay Hitler rejected the offer for no convincing reason. He talked about the need to take Hungarian and Polish claims into account, he questioned the reliability of the Czechs and he protested loudly at 'intolerable' Czech treatment of Sudeten Germans. If war was to be avoided, German troops must occupy the Sudetenland at once. Before Chamberlain left for London on 23 September Hitler handed him a memorandum in which he demanded the evacuation of the Sudetenland between 26 and 28 September. Chamberlain protested angrily at the 'ultimatum', a description which the Führer blandly contested. The temperature rose sharply when news came of Czech mobilization. Angry exchanges followed Hitler's comment that the affair was 'settled' as the Czechs would now make no concessions. Finally, after a despairing Chamberlain decided to return home, Hitler relented slightly and extended the time limit for evacuation of the Sudetenland to 1 October, a 'concession' with which he made great play although it had not the slightest bearing on his military plans. Back home Chamberlain found his colleagues less impressed by the Führer's magnanimity. On 25 September the British government decided that it could not advise Czechoslovakia to accept Hitler's demands. When France heard that Czechoslovakia had rejected the Godesberg ultimatum, she affirmed her intention of aiding the Czechs if war came, and mobilized fourteen divisions. On 26 September a reluctant Chamberlain promised to support France if she had to aid the Czechs.

Why did Hitler precipitate this new and graver crisis? Presented with the Sudetenland 'on a plate', as Hitler put it later, he preferred to engineer a deadlock and play for time in the hope that he might secure the whole of Czechoslovakia at one bite. A more difficult question is whether he intended to attain his objective by war or not. It has been suggested that Hitler was bluffing throughout, that he deliberately went to the very edge of the precipice but never intended to fall over it.[16] That is far too rational an explanation of his conduct. For as Halder once said of Hitler: 'attempts to try and explain beyond all question on the basis of his words and deeds the enigmatical dictator who fitted into no ordinary scheme of things . . . must in the final resort remain just as inadequate as the attempts of contemporaries to understand clearly his innermost thoughts and the particular stage decisions, evolving in his mind, had reached.'[17]

One clue to understanding Hitler's attitude during the Czech crisis lies in his whole attitude to war.[18] War was not a sign of bankrupt statesmanship to the Führer, a hopeless plunge into the irrational but, on the contrary, a sign of national virility and a natural extension of the struggle for existence in which all living beings were engaged. That instinctive aversion to war widespread in the western democracies was totally lacking in Hitler. He told the Hungarian premier and his foreign secretary on 20 September that he would press the German demands 'with brutal frankness' at Godesberg; if disturbances occurred in Czechoslovakia he would commence military operations and eliminate this 'aircraft carrier' in the heart of Europe. One might well conclude from this and similar remarks to Lipski, the Polish ambassador, that Hitler was bent on war at all costs.[19] No doubt his instincts were for war because he sensed that with appeasement in the air the complete destruction of Czechoslovakia could only be brought about by military action. But being naturally devious and cautious in his tactics, he preferred to keep the options open as long as possible. For he knew that if the western powers lost their nerve and capitulated – and he warned the Hungarians that the Czechs might submit 'to every demand' – it would be difficult to resist a peaceful solution out of regard for public opinion in Germany. However undesirable a settlement would be – because the Czech problem

[16] A. Taylor, *The Origins of the Second World War* (London, 1961), pp. 167, 183.

[17] Quoted in A. Hillgruber, *op. cit.*, p. 24.

[18] Cf. highly revealing and neglected *OKW* memorandum 19 April 1938, *IMT*, XXXVIII, pp. 48–50.

[19] A recently-published diary confirms this impression: H. Groscurth, *Tagebücher eines Abwehroffiziers, 1938–1940* (Stuttgart, 1970), pp. 104, 109, 111–12, 114, 117, 127.

as such would remain unresolved as he told Lipski – still, he would at least have the consolation of an ostentatious military promenade into the Sudetenland to pay Benes out for his 'obstructionism' in May. Either way Hitler stood to gain. Free of Chamberlain's embrace, he could move forward ready for war, eager for it even, but not irrevocably committed to it if the situation changed.

One thing is certain: Germany was ready for war in 1938. Not for a general war, of course, because Hitler was perfectly well aware that shortages of essential raw materials and reserves of only 500,000 men made the hit-and-run strategy of the bank robber mandatory for Germany. From 1933 onwards he had resolutely opposed the defence-in-depth strategy of the General Thomas school, not because he failed to appreciate the force of their arguments, but simply because that strategy would strain Germany's resources to breaking-point. Also, a defence-in-depth strategy with the corollary of high-level investment in the armaments industry and long-term economic reorganization would slow down the pace of rearmament in the short term; that meant the abandonment of an expansionist foreign policy for the foreseeable future. Instead, Hitler opted quite deliberately for a defence-in-breadth strategy, i.e. rapid expansion of the army in order to realize his territorial ambitions at the earliest possible moment either by diplomatic intimidation or by *Blitzkrieg* methods.

Precisely because Hitler was so acutely aware of the discrepancy between Germany's material resources and his own far-reaching ambitions, he attached great importance to psychological warfare in the furtherance of his plans. Revolutionary propaganda, as he told Rauschning in 1932, would bombard and demoralize opponents as surely as artillery fire had done in the First World War and without the terrible carnage of that conflict (for he had no wish to sacrifice German youth needlessly). The demagogic techniques developed in the internal political battles of the 1920s were applied to international affairs in the 1930s. Lies, deceit, blatant misrepresentation and shameless exploitation of lacunae in an enemy's armour – the moral commitment of the west to self-determination is the most obvious example – formed an integral part of Hitler's technique of conquest.

In this context the German minorities scattered throughout Central and Eastern Europe had an important role to play as 'fifth columns' or centres of subversion undermining the citadel from within. Before 1937 Hitler displayed little interest in these minorities. The *Volksdeutsche Rat*, set up in 1933, acted only as a liaison body keeping them in touch with Berlin. In 1937 Hitler's attitude changed. In February Werner Lorenz, a high-ranking *SS* officer, was put in charge of the *Volksdeutsche Mittelstelle* and orders were given that it must be consulted on all minority questions. In the past Hitler had avoided commitment to competing factions in the minorities. In July 1938 he finally conferred full authority on Lorenz to issue binding directives to the minorities, a sure sign that they were now to be exploited ruthlessly in the interests of Nazi imperialism, as the case of the Sudeten Germans amply illustrates.

Finally, in connection with the *Blitzkrieg* it should be noted that Hitler's technique of conquest was coupled with a naïvely simple but brutal theory of exploitation. At the height of the war Hitler spelt it out with unmistakable clarity in private conversation. It was not just a matter of seizing supplies from a defeated state to prepare for the next campaign. The long-term policy was to hold wages and prices in conquered territories at a low level and permanently exploit the non-German labour force in order to maintain German living standards. Because the spoils of war would far exceed Germany's financial outlay, Hitler never worried about rearmament costs or later war costs: 'no state has ever gone bankrupt for economic reasons', he observed triumphantly to Finance Minister von Krosigk, 'but only as a result of losing a war'.[20] The implication was clear; economic stresses and strains generated by rapid rearmament were regarded by Hitler as a calculated risk in the long-term interests of German imperialism. Economic difficulties may have made him accelerate the tempo of his foreign policy – though in the nature of things there is no direct evidence of this – but most certainly politico-strategic ambitions were the decisive factor in the complex equation.

When senior generals expressed grave misgivings about Hitler's plans in the summer of 1938, this was because they assumed that an attack on Czechoslovakia would lead to a major war involving Britain, France and possibly Russia. Such a conflict could end only in the defeat of Germany. It is unnecessary to dwell on the point which is not in dispute. Summarized briefly, the major

[20] *Hitler's Table Talk, 1941–1944*, p. 635; cf. p. 460.

weaknesses in the German position, as the generals saw it, were: firstly, a shortage of raw materials which made prolonged warfare extremely hazardous; secondly, the airforce, having been designed primarily to support the field army, was incapable either then or in 1939 of carrying out strategic bombing of enemy territory; and, finally, in the event of a French attack, the West Wall could only be held for a few days, as Hitler knew despite his blustering confidence.

Hitler brushed these weighty objections aside because he operated on the different assumption that Britain and France would not intervene; nor did he expect Russian intervention either. If he was right – and his intuitive judgment had been impressively vindicated in 1936 – then Germany's strategy made good sense. Only five divisions were ordered to guard the West Wall; three were left in East Prussia largely because their movement would attract attention; and the bulk of the army, some thirty-seven divisions including three armed and four motorized divisions to form the spearhead of the attack, was deployed around Czechoslovakia in a ring from Silesia to Austria. Against Keitel's assertion at Nuremberg that the army could not have pierced the Czech defences – and that, therefore, aggression had never been intended – must be set the fact that at the secret meeting called by Brauchitsch on 4 August the *Wehrkreis* commanders agreed that the training and equipment of their troops, though insufficient to wage war on two fronts, was probably adequate for the defeat of Czechoslovakia.[21] A historian of the period has observed quite rightly that 'the threat to Czechoslovakia was real and based on ready force but as regards England and France it was a policy of bluff and bluster'.[22]

This is a convenient point at which to examine the relationship between economic factors and the Czech crisis. As indicated earlier, there is no direct evidence that Hitler's awareness of the deteriorating economic situation exerted influence on his policy. There is, however, abundant evidence that his determination to

[21] R. O'Neill, *op. cit.*, p. 158; cf. *DBFP*, III, appendix III, British military attaché's report, p. 626.

[22] Telford Taylor, *Sword and Swastika. The Wehrmacht in the Third Reich* (London, 1953), p. 222. Cf. *DBFP*, III, ii, appendix I, 9 September 1938. Sir Nevile Henderson: 'Hitler's position is that of a man bluffing with a full house in his hand. If his bluff fails he will show his full house, not throw in his hand.'

destroy Czechoslovakia influenced economic development. In April 1938, when he ordered an acceleration of the building of the West Wall, the switching of 300,000 men from the building industry exacerbated an already difficult labour situation. Labour discipline was fraying at the edges in the winter of 1937/8; according to one authority workers at I.G. Farben's Wolfen works were openly absenting themselves to visit the cinema while others got drunk during the morning break.[23] The wage spiral assumed menacing proportions in industries vital to rearmament and pirating of skilled labour was increasing. Under cover of the Czech crisis Goering plucked up courage and acted. Two important decrees were issued in June 1938. The first authorized labour trustees to fix maxima for wage rates in certain designated industries, with fines or imprisonment for infringement of regulations. The second decree introduced compulsory labour service for all workers, making them liable to conscription for work of national importance. These decrees were unpopular with the working class and were not rigidly enforced. In pactice wage regulation proved immensely difficult. Few employers were punished perhaps because they avoided the issue by extending fringe benefits instead. All the same, a milestone had been passed. The Nazis had taken the first hesitant steps towards open coercion in the field of labour relations, and despite what has been said about cautious enforcement of the decrees, they were not without some effect on the situation.

Another event of great importance occurred in June 1938 when the aims of the Four Year Plan were altered. By the summer it was quite clear that the discrepancy between target and performance was very considerable. Early in 1937 Hitler realized that economic mobilization would take not four but six years, i.e. Germany would be ready for war in 1942, not 1940 as he had demanded in the 1936 memorandum. That view was shared by high command circles and explains why he talked in November 1937 of solving the living space problem by 1942/3 at the latest. That Hitler took no action to accelerate economic mobilization for another eighteen months was probably due to the confidence he reposed in Goering. The latter was extremely loathe to face up to the stark alternatives; either to preserve the wider aims of the

[23] T. W. Mason, 'Labour in the Third Reich, 1933–1939' in *Past and Present*, 1966, p. 132.

plan and curtail rearmament or to maintain (and increase) the tempo of rearmament by abandoning the non-military parts of the plan. Probably Goering would have equivocated indefinitely had it not been for the Sudeten crisis. As war loomed closer, the unsatisfactory progress on the military side became a cause of grave anxiety. In mid-June Goering decided to abandon the wider aims and concentrate instead on the production of certain war materials: explosives and gunpowder (where Goering described the position as 'catastrophic'), fuel, aluminium, *buna* and ores. On 12 July Goering confirmed Krauch's six-year *Wehrwirtschaftlicher Neuer Erzeugungsplan* for the improvement of production in respect of these raw materials. As the international crisis deepened, the plan became an emergency plan on 12 August as far as powder, explosives and vital chemicals were concerned, and as such remained in force until the outbreak of war. It is not without significance that army command and I.G. Farben now aimed at attaining maximum production of these items by the end of 1939. Autarky in the wider sense had been abandoned. The German economy was at last on a war footing with military autarky as the sole objective.[24] That was not necessarily a victory for the army. On the contrary, the appointment of special commissioners in various branches of the war economy sharply reduced army influence over production processes. The real victor was I.G. Farben whose influence grew by leaps and bounds in 1938. The new plan with its ambitions targets was practically an I.G. Farben plan; two-thirds of the investment was absorbed by this giant concern, its links with the government became extremely close and many of its directors occupied key positions in the economic hierarchy.

We return now to the situation after the Godesberg meeting. The tension reached new heights on 26 September after Hitler's *Sportspalast* speech, a tirade of unprecedented violence in which he succeeded in reducing the issue of war and peace to a personal confrontation with Benes, the Czech 'sneaking about through the world' while the Führer did his duty 'as a decent German soldier'.

---

[24] By 1938 German military expenditure amounted to 17,200 million *RM*, 17 per cent of the GNP compared with 13 per cent in 1937. Cf. thorough discussion in B. Carroll, *Design for Total War. Arms and economics in the Third Reich* (The Hague/Paris, 1968), Chapter X.

The issue put to the enraptured crowds was a simple one: either Benes accepted the terms by 2 p.m. on 28 September and gave the Sudeten Germans their freedom, or 'we will go and fetch this freedom for ourselves'. Visited by Sir Horace Wilson, Chamberlain's personal envoy, the next morning Hitler remained utterly intransigent. Asked by Wilson what would happen if the Czechs rejected the ultimatum, he retorted with relish that he would destroy Czechoslovakia. Wilson's solemn warning that France and Britain would aid Czechoslovakia did not sober him. Immediately afterwards Hitler ordered the spearhead of the assault, seven divisions (three armed and four motorised), to take up advanced positions near the Czech frontier. They were to be ready to attack on 30 September. A few hours later mobilization of the five regular western divisions was ordered.

War seemed inevitable. Yet already on 27 September Hitler was wavering. Watching a motorized division roll through Berlin, he was angered by the silence and sparseness of the crowds. Turning away from the window, he snapped irritably that he could not wage war 'with people like these.'[25] Equally alarming was the report of the German military attaché in Paris, who stated that the partial mobilization ordered in Paris on 24 September was so thorough that by the sixth day of a general mobilization sixty-five divisions might well be deployed along the German frontier. The attaché believed, quite erroneously, that France planned to launch an offensive from Lower Alsace and Lorraine. Meanwhile Czech mobilization, ordered on 22 September, was complete. What it meant was that the vital element of surprise to which Hitler had pinned his hopes was a rapidly dwindling asset. General war seemed distinctly possible. Faced with this prospect, Hitler's natural caution gradually reasserted itself. The first sign of uncertainty was his approval of a conciliatory draft reply to Chamberlain's letter of the previous day. While conceding not one iota in the cause of peace, the letter defended the German position in more restrained language than usual, stated that Germany only wanted the Sudetenland, and invited Chamberlain to continue his efforts to bring the Czechs to their senses.[26]

[25] E. Kordt, *Nicht aus den Akten. Die Wilhelmstrasse in Frieden und Krieg* (Stuttgart, 1950), p. 268.

[26] That was not the turning-point in the crisis, for on the night of 27–8 September Hitler was still talking belligerently of war; L. Hill, 'Three crises, 1938–39'; *JCH*, 1966, pp. 118–19.

Chamberlain responded eagerly, assuring Hitler that he could get all the essentials without war and without delay. Before that reply reached Berlin Hitler finally edged away from the precipice. Tension was at its height on 28 September as the ultimatum ran out. Hitler wandered about the chancellery talking belligerently to anyone he happened to buttonhole but filled with growing doubts about the advisability of war. Several factors probably conspired together at this point to force his hand. News arrived of the mobilization of the British fleet the previous evening, another worrying sign that general war might be imminent. Then François-Poncet presented his government's new plan for the surrender of the Sudetenland. Hitler seemed impressed as he listened to the ambassador's spirited representations and saw from the map that the area to be ceded was considerably greater than that offered by Chamberlain. In the midst of the interview Attolico, the Italian ambassador, brought an urgent message from Mussolini who asked for a postponement of military action for twenty-four hours in order to consider new proposals from London and Paris (which Hitler had just seen). Goering and Neurath urged acceptance of the request. The ring of peace closed round the Führer and somewhat hesitantly he agreed to Attolico's request. By the time Henderson arrived with Chamberlain's letter, Hitler had made up his mind. Just before the time limit for Czech acceptance expired at 2 p.m., Britain, France and Italy were invited to attend a conference at Munich the following day.

The news was greeted with relief all over Europe. Whether it signified an 'irrevocable' decision on Hitler's part is less certain. The Führer was in an excited and belligerent mood when he joined Mussolini on the train *en route* for Munich. Reminding the Duce that they would have to fight the western powers one day – and the sooner the better before Germany was encircled – he described in detail his plans for destroying Czechoslovakia. According to Ciano's diary Hitler was only persuaded with difficulty to await the outcome of the conference. At the outset he insisted that the purpose of the conference was simply to find a way of giving Germany the Sudetenland by 1 October. What followed was an abject surrender recounted elsewhere. It was finally agreed that the Sudetenland be occupied in stages between 1 and 10 October; that plebiscites be held in disputed areas; and, after Hungarian and Polish claims had been met, the four powers would guarantee the rump Czech state.

There is abundant evidence that Hitler was displeased with the Munich Conference. The role of peacemaker was irksome to a man determined to be beholden to no one. In the conference chamber he scowled and sat in silence most of the time. When Chamberlain visited him in his Munich flat on 30 September the Führer was moody and preoccupied. Somewhat reluctantly he signed an Anglo-German declaration stating the resolve of the two peoples never to go to war again, but clearly attached no importance to the piece of paper which Chamberlain waved to the crowds at Heston airport. Back in Berlin, when congratulated on the conference, he snapped irritably: 'That fellow Chamberlain has spoiled my entry into Prague.'[27] Hitler's interpreter, Paul Schmidt, commented that the Führer failed to grasp the full extent of his victory over the western powers. The reason is not far to seek. In January 1939 Hitler explained to Colonel Beck, the Polish foreign minister, that the surprising offer by Chamberlain and Daladier deflected him from a purely political solution which would have been tantamount to liquidating Czechoslovakia, and had obliged him to settle instead for the ethnographical solution. Repeating the argument to the Hungarian foreign minister he blamed the Magyars for having looked at the Czech problem ethnographically instead of from a 'territorial' (i.e. strategic) point of view. If Hungary had joined in at the right moment he could have 'laughed in Chamberlain's face'.[28] He continued to regret the 'capitulation' until the end of his days; in 1945 he complained to Bormann that by surrendering, the west made it difficult for him to sieze the initiative and commence hostilities but he ought to have gone to war and had he done so would have won a swift victory.

The complete destruction of Czechoslovakia clearly remained Hitler's objective. Already on 21 October the army was ordered to be ready to liquidate Czechoslovakia by a surprise attack. Serious opposition from Britain and France was hardly likely judging by their waning interest in the Czechs. Accordingly the army was instructed on 17 December to prepare for the occupa-

[27] *IMT*, XII, p. 531.
[28] *DGFP*, D, V, no. 272. This was certainly not the reason for the peaceful outcome of the crisis but may possibly have been intended to warn the Hungarians off the Carpatho-Ukraine.

tion of Czechoslovakia on the assumption that there would be no resistance.

To disrupt the Czech state from within Hitler found a non-German 'fifth column': the Slovaks. Immediately after Munich the Germans encouraged Slovak aspirations for greater autonomy. In mid-October Goering assured two Slovak ministers of German support for an independent Slovakia adding the ominous comment: 'air bases in Slovakia for an operation against the east . . . very important'.[29] Hitler probably decided in January 1939 to occupy Czechoslovakia sometime in the spring, possibly because negotiations with Poland were proving abortive. On 12 February 1939 he received Tuka, the Slovak nationalist leader, in audience and encouraged agitation for complete independence. Simultaneously his attitude to the Czechs hardened. Psychological warfare commenced in January when Chvalkovsky, the Czech foreign minister, alarmed by rumours of impending German action, hurried to Berlin for reassurance. He was bullied as Schuschnigg had been bullied in 1938. The Czechs must mend their ways, reduce their army, accept German direction of their foreign policy and outlaw the Jews, insisted the irate Führer.

The Czechs only anticipated Hitler's action by a few days. On 9/10 March President Hacha, in a last despairing attempt to maintain the integrity of his country, dismissed the Slovak government and proclaimed martial law. The Germans promptly applied pressure to the Slovaks. Ex-premier Tiso was flown to Berlin and warned by Hitler that unless he proclaimed Slovakian independence immediately his country would be swallowed up by the greedy Hungarians massing their troops on the frontier. Tiso agreed. On 14 March Slovakia declared its independence and Czechoslovakia ceased to exist.

Meanwhile Hacha and Chvalkovsky hurried to Berlin to save something from the wreckage. They were bullied unmercifully by Hitler, Ribbentrop and Goering until Hacha, physically and mentally exhausted, asked Germany to 'protect' the Czech people. 'Children', Hitler exclaimed excitedly as his secretaries kissed him, 'this is the greatest day of my life. I shall go down in history as the greatest German.'[30] There was no need to devastate 'beautiful

[29] *DGFP*, D, IV, no. 68.
[30] A. Zoller, *Hitler privat. Erlebnisbericht seiner Geheimsekretärin* (Düsseldorf, 1949), p. 84.

Prague' by aerial bombardment as Goering had threatened.[31] The citadel had again fallen from within. When seventeen divisions moved into Bohemia and Moravia on 15 March ostensibly it was by Czech invitation. Hitler spent the night in Hradcin castle and next day issued a proclamation establishing the protectorate of Bohemia and Moravia 'part of the *Lebensraum* of the German people for over a thousand years'. On 16 March in response to Tiso's telegram, thoughtfully drafted by the Germans, 'independent' Slovakia was occupied by three divisions and placed under German protection. At this point Hitler's interest in 'national independence' ceased: when Ruthenia proclaimed its independence and appealed to Hitler, the Führer was strangely silent. By prior arrangement with Hungary Magyar troops occupied Ruthenia and the dismemberment of Czechoslovakia was complete.

Hitler's entry into Prague shifted the military balance decisively in Germany's favour in Eastern Europe. By straightening out the line from the southern tip of Silesia to the northern point of the *Ostmark*, Hitler succeeded in driving a wedge between Poland and Hungary preventing any possibility of joint co-operation against Germany. If Hitler had designs on Poland, he was now in a much stronger position to impose his will on her. Germany commanded the approaches to Cracow, Limberg and the Ukraine, and the airforce was only twenty-five minutes flying time from Polish industrial centres. The Little Entente was smashed beyond repair. If it came to war with Britain she had little chance now of finding eastern allies, so that the effects of a British blockade could be easily offset.

The economic gains were considerable. Czech industrial potential represented a significant addition to the German war machine; between them Austria and Czechoslovakia added three million tons of steel capacity to Germany's twenty-three million tons. The Skoda armaments works at Pilsen and the Brno small arms factory were valuable prizes. Much military equipment fell into German hands including 2,200 guns, 600 tanks and 750 aircraft. German industry and banking quickly obtained a dominant position in the Czech economy. For the next six years the area was systematically exploited by the Germans who extracted raw

[31] Hitler revealed later that the threat was a hollow one as thick fog grounded all aircraft: *Hitler's Table Talk, 1941–1944*, p. 204.

materials from it without straining their own balance of payments.

The wider economic consequences were even more important. From the *Anschluss* onwards Germany began to exert a dominant influence over the economic life of the Danubian basin. With the Four Year Plan Nazi interest in the exploitation of the Balkans steadily increased. Their aim was no longer the negotiation of simple barter agreements but the creation of a *Grossraumwirtschaft* in which Yugoslavia, Bulgaria and Roumania would become dependent territories producing raw materials needed by the *Reich*. By 1937 Germany was not only taking grain and ores from the area but investing capital to produce what Germany needed, e.g. German investment in Yugoslavia rose from fifty-five million dinars in 1934 to 820 million dinars in 1938. It was indicative of growing Nazi dependence upon Balkan sources of supply that in September 1938 Goering admitted frankly that the success of the Four Year Plan was bound up with the political expansion of the Reich in South-eastern Europe.

CHAPTER SIX

The Road to War, 1939

AT the Hossbach Conference one of Hitler's most compelling arguments for a forward policy was a lively fear that Germany's military superiority was a declining asset. This point was brought home forcibly to him immediately after the Munich Conference when Britain announced an acceleration of her rearmament programme. Hitler was deeply angered by the news. Even before the Sudetenland occupation was complete, he had ordered a massive increase in German armaments. On 14 October Goering informed the air ministry of Hitler's decision to increase the air-force fivefold, speed up naval expansion and provide more tanks and heavy guns for the army.

This was no momentary flash of anger on Hitler's part. In late October he sought a formal alliance with Italy. Possibly a desire to pin the restless Italians down played some part in this move. But basically Hitler knew that the balance of power would not remain in Germany's favour long, now that Britain had to be counted as an irreconcilable foe. *Gauleiter* Forster recounted a revealing remark of Hitler's in the autumn of 1938 to the effect that within two years, 'the others' would be stronger than Germany.[1] The implication was clear: Germany could not wait until 1942/3 'at the latest' (the Hossbach timetable) to seize living space she must act no later than 1940/41 (the timetable in the 1936 memorandum). This sobering thought gave an added urgency to Hitler's post-Munich policy. Accelerated rearmament plus a military alliance with Italy were essential steps for maintaining Germany's present military advantage and preparing her for every eventuality.

[1] *DBFP*, III, iii, appendix VI; cf. similar comments on 10 February 1939 in H. Groscurth, *op. cit.*, p. 167.

Hitler told Mussolini in March 1940 that a comparison of the relative military strengths of Germany and her opponents decided him in favour of war. '. . . the conditions of the struggle would, in two years time, at best not have been more favourable for Germany.' *Ciano's Diplomatic Papers*, p. 361.

Hitler's policy towards Austria and Czechoslovakia was determined largely by strategic considerations. Until these countries were firmly under German control, Germany could not dominate Central and South-eastern Europe. What followed next was less obvious. There is some evidence that Hitler was uncertain in the winter of 1938–9 whether to continue in an easterly direction or strike quickly at Britain and France. If he decided on the former course, several possibilities existed. On the basis of German press comment on the economic value of the Ukraine at the end of 1938, some observers thought that Hitler might be contemplating a sudden attack on Russia, a conjecture for which there seems to have been no foundation. Others thought that Carpatho-Ukraine might be used as a base by Nazi propagandists to agitate for the creation of a Ukrainian state under German control. That possibility was ruled out, temporarily at any rate, when Hitler allowed Hungary to occupy the area in March 1939. With the entry into Prague and the recovery of the Memelland whatever doubts he had were finally resolved. Hitler was set on an easterly course and it became a matter of urgency to determine German policy towards Poland.

The existence of a German minority in the so-called Polish Corridor and the separation of Danzig from the *Reich* were grievances which could easily be exploited if it was Hitler's intention to destroy Poland. At first, however, Hitler's determination to settle accounts with Poland was outweighed by hopes of turning her into a friendly satellite, even into an ally for the war against Russia. For contemptuous though he was of Slav 'sub-humans', he never felt for the Poles the keen dislike he had for the Czechs. As we have seen earlier, he admired Pilsudski and often referred to Poland as a 'bulwark against bolshevism'. Polish indifference to the *Anschluss* and her eager participation in the dismemberment of Czechoslovakia were encouraging signs that Poland might come to terms with Germany.

In October 1938 Ribbentrop opened up a serious dialogue with Poland by requesting the return of Danzig, the creation of an extra-territorial corridor for German use and Polish accession to the Anti-Comintern Pact. When Colonel Beck, the Polish foreign minister, replied in the negative, Hitler tried summit diplomacy. On 5 January 1939 Beck was invited to the Berghof. For once Hitler did not employ the tactics of intimidation used on

Schuschnigg, Tiso and Hacha. Quite the reverse. The Führer
hinted at the possibility of liquidating Czechoslovakia by agree-
ment with all interested parties of which Poland was one. He went
further, stating categorically that Germany had no interest in the
Ukraine, an area eyed greedily by the Poles. The next day
Ribbentrop spelt it out in detail for Beck. Once Danzig and the
Corridor were settled, Germany would support Polish aspirations
in the Ukraine. On 26 January Ribbentrop repeated the offer.
Beck readily admitted to an interest in the Ukraine and Black
Sea areas, but expressed fear of the possible effects a new Polish–
German agreement might have on Russia. Quite certainly Hitler's
offer was more than a tactical manœuvre to allay Polish fears
about the destruction of Czechoslovakia. Proof of this is contained
in Ribbentrop's instructions to the ambassador in Warsaw on
23 March for his forthcoming interview with Beck. Hitler, said
Ribbentrop, wanted a settlement of Danzig soon, out of concern for
the general political situation. Great possibilities existed in Polish–
German co-operation: 'above all Germany could then pursue
a common eastern policy with Poland in which the identical interests of both countries in warding off bolshevism could also effectively be realized'.[2] Germany would allow Poland to play a leading
role in the Ukraine and would be accommodating over Slovakia.
But, he concluded ominously, there were limits to Germany's
patience. If the Poles were still passive or evasive, the Führer
was resolved to withdraw his offer at once. A satellite Poland
could become, equal partnership with Germany did not arise.

This ominous tone was re-echoed on 25 March during Hitler's
briefing session with Brauchitsch. In keeping with present policy,
the Führer declared that he did not intend to solve the Danzig
question by force. Even so, doubts about the chances of a peaceful
solution were already stirring in his mind as the season for military
action opened in the spring. To be on the safe side, Brauchitsch
was instructed to begin work on the Polish problem. And Hitler
added that, if especially favourable circumstances did arise in the
near future, Poland would have to be 'so beaten down that,
during the next few decades, she need not be taken into account
as a political factor. In a solution of this kind the Führer envisaged
an advanced frontier extending from the eastern border of East
Prussia to the eastern tip of Silesia.'[3]

[2] *DGFP*, D, VI, no. 73.   [3] *Ibid.*, no. 99.

The next day Hitler's doubts were amply confirmed by Beck's reply to renewed German demands. While still prepared to negotiate over Danzig and the Corridor, Beck flatly refused to surrender the city, and the Polish ambassador in Berlin warned Ribbentrop that attempts to take it by force meant war. Thus before the British guarantee was given to Poland on 31 March, Hitler's patience had worn perilously thin. On hearing of the guarantee, he exploded with rage: 'I'll cook them a stew that they'll choke on', he shouted as he thumped his marble-topped desk.[4] The next day, 1 April, speaking at Wilhelmshaven at the launching of the battleship *Tirpitz*, he upbraided Britain for interfering in matters which did not concern her, and warned Poland that powers trying to pull chestnuts out of the fire for the western powers would burn their fingers. On 3 April the army was ordered to draw up operational plans by 1 May for an attack on Poland (*Plan White*) to be carried out at any time from 1 September.

Admittedly, in the directive of 11 April outlining the tasks of the armed forces for 1939/40, Hitler did express himself cautiously.[5] Relations with Poland would, he said, continue to be based on the principle of avoiding trouble. A final reckoning would only be necessary if the Poles changed their attitude towards Germany. And even if it came to war, he would isolate Poland if possible and crush her by 'sudden heavy blows'. He even minimized the importance of *Plan White* saying that it was only a 'precautionary complement' to Germany's military preparations against the west; it was not to be looked upon as a 'necessary prerequisite' of a military conflict with the west. These remarks are not, however, evidence of indecision; more likely they represent a calculated attempt on Hitler's part to allay the fears of senior officers and avoid a repetition of the opposition encountered over Czechoslovakia. For that reason he by-passed the high command from the start and dealt directly with army command. No doubt he calculated that senior officers would more readily obey the Führer's personal orders rather than those of the high command whose intervention in planning was generally resented.

[4] H. B. Gisevius, *To the Bitter End* (London, 1948), p. 362. The German is more dramatic: *Denen werde ich einen Teufelstrank brauen.*

[5] *DGFP*, D, VI, no. 185.

While military planning went ahead, psychological warfare to soften up the enemy – always an important ingredient in Hitler's campaigns – commenced at the end of the month. On 28 April 1939 in a Reichstag speech Hitler denounced the Anglo–German Convention on the grounds that Britain was now seeking to encircle Germany; he also denounced the Non-Aggression Pact of 1934 because the Poles, so he argued, had rejected 'reasonable' German demands and were conspiring against the *Reich*. Simultaneously Goebbels's propaganda machine swung into action with a predictably mendacious campaign to arouse public opinion against the Poles, not a difficult task in Germany where the eastern frontiers were bitterly resented by Germans of practically all political persuasions.

The British guarantee taken in conjunction with Beck's refusal to give way removed lingering doubts from Hitler's mind. Once again opposition to his will evoked 'a wilful determination to be committed'.[6] From April onwards he relied on the well-tried techniques of coercion to to get his way. What one cannot be absolutely certain about is whether he opted deliberately and 'irrevocably' for war, completely excluding any possibility of accommodation with Poland. On the face of it that seems inconsistent with what we know of the Führer's changeable moods and wily tactics. Yet there is no compelling evidence to suggest that he seriously supposed another Munich likely. The truth surely is that he knew only too well that room for manœuvre was dwindling rapidly as western opposition to his policies grew after the entry into Prague. That conviction underlay much of what he had to say at the conference held on 23 May.

On the day before the conference a formal alliance with Italy, the so-called Pact of Steel, was signed in Berlin amidst great pomp and splendour. The Axis Powers had finally entered into binding military commitments which relieved Hitler of the fear (so he supposed) that Italy would lose heart when the crunch came as she had done in September 1938. On 23 May a confident Führer addressed twelve senior officers together with Raeder and Goering on the subject of the Polish campaign, detailed plans for which were submitted by Brauchitsch and Halder. Notes of the speech were taken unofficially by Adjutant Schmundt.[7]

[6] F. H. Hinsley, *op. cit.*, p. 12.
[7] *DGFP*, D, VI, no. 433.

To impress his captive audience with the need for action in the near future, Hitler put Poland in the wider setting of Germany's growing economic difficulties. The argument was that Germany could not acquiesce in the present balance of world economic power. 'Circumstances must rather be adapted to meet the demands', and that meant the invasion of other states. 'Living space proportionate to the greatness of the state is fundamental to every power. One can do without it for a time but sooner or later the problems will have to be solved by hook or by crook. The alternatives are rise or decline. In 15 to 20 years' time the solution will be forced upon us. No German statesman can shirk the problem for longer.' Apart from the time-scale, which had suddenly lengthened (and it has to be admitted that Hitler was often careless about figures) the argument was the old familiar one. 'It is not Danzig that is at stake,' he exclaimed in a much-quoted passage, 'For us it is a matter of expanding our living space in the east and making food supplies secure and also solving the problem of the Baltic states. Food supplies can only be obtained from thinly populated areas. Over and above fertility, the thorough German cultivation will tremendously increase the produce.' Whether Poland itself would provide the necessary living space or whether it was only an intermediate station on the road eastwards, was not clear probably because Hitler himself did not know the answer at that stage. What was clearly demonstrated was his determination to destroy Poland 'at the first suitable opportunity', if only for reasons of national security: she was an unreliable barrier against bolshevism (so he now decided) and she was likely to attack Germany in the rear should war break out in the west. This time war was certain[8] – 'further successes can no longer be won without bloodshed' – and he warned his audience that there would be no 'repetition of Czechia'.

What he was unsure about was how the west would react to an attack on Poland. 'The problem "Poland" cannot be dissociated from the showdown with the west', he remarked sensibly enough, '. . . our task is to isolate Poland. Success in isolating her will be decisive . . . it must not come to a simultaneous showdown with the west.' So crucial was this, that if it was not certain that the west would not declare war during an eastern campaign, then war must be waged against the west in the first instance. This he

[8] Strictly speaking 'there will be fighting'.

immediately contradicted by saying that it would be better to
attack in the west and settle Poland simultaneously, i.e. the very
war he was supposedly anxious to avoid.

Hitler's remarks about the strategy to be adopted against
Britain merit closer examination. At first he spoke of defeating
her by a 'few devastating blows'. But though he strongly advocated
the *Blitzkrieg* strategy if at all feasible, he was aware that a surprise
attack on the British fleet was unlikely to succeed after 1940/41
for by that time British anti-aircraft defences would be considerably improved.

Therefore he advanced an alternative plan for dealing with
Britain. This posited the seizure of bases in the Low Countries
and in France from which a greatly-strengthened navy and airforce, working in collaboration, would hammer at British lines of
communication with the outside world. In this connection he
spoke of war lasting ten to fifteen years before Britain was finally
brought to her knees. For such a conflict preparations must be
made owing to the uncertainty of a *Blitzkrieg* succeeding in the
case of Britain.

At first sight talk of a long war seems totally inconsistent with
all that has been said about Hitler's commitment to the *Blitzkrieg*.
At Nuremberg Raeder argued that this wild talk was intended to
justify a proposal slipped in at the very end of the speech for the
establishment at armed forces high command of a special planning
staff consisting of representatives from the three branches of the
armed forces but under Hitler's personal command. In fact, the
proposal was merely part of Hitler's sustained effort to keep the
commanders-in-chief on his side. Nothing whatsoever was done
to implement it. Hence we can discount Raeder's thesis that the
speech was an elaborate charade to conceal one solitary objective
(never implemented).

The truth is that Hitler was already looking beyond the
Blitzkrieg era to the day when Germany dominated the continent
– which he assumed she could do without British interference.
When that day came Germany would command the resources
of the continent from the Atlantic to the Ural mountains and
could then take on Britain in the crucial battle for world hegemony which he had not expected to have to fight at the beginning
of his political career. Britain's refusal to entertain a German
alliance and her mounting opposition to German expansion

probably convinced Hitler that the historic struggle would occur in his lifetime, possibly in a few years.

All the same, he did not expect this war to break out in the near future. In January 1939 he approved the so-called Z Plan which gave absolute priority to the building of a huge fleet including ten battleships, three battle cruisers and four heavy cruisers. This plan proves that Hitler had lost confidence in the ability of the airforce to deal a knock-out blow at Britain, as he seems to have thought possible in 1938. Until the new plan was completed in 1946, Germany had to avoid war with Britain as Raeder was well aware. When Hitler authorized the plan he was looking ahead to the time when Germany dominated Europe and would require a powerful fleet to defeat Britain. That was why in reply to Goering's question at the end of the conference on 23 May, Hitler declared that the naval programme would go ahead as planned, i.e. there was no need to accelerate it because he did not expect war with Britain. War with Poland was a different matter.

If Hitler supposed for one moment that Poland would give way after the denunciation of the Non-Aggression Pact, the firm Polish reply on 5 May dashed such hopes. After the Reichstag speech on 28 April Hitler lapsed into complete silence towards official Poland, retreated to the Berghof for the summer and made no attempt to approach Poland until the very eve of war (and that for propaganda purposes). It can, of couse, be argued that these tactics, which placed the ball back in the Polish court, were best suited to Hitler's purpose: and allowed him to reserve final judgment on war and peac : until the last possible moment.

If he seemed indifferent t>wards Polish reactions, for whatever reason, he undoubtedly kej t a close and critical eye on military preparations for her destruction. By mid-June *Plan White* was ready. The plan was to launch simultaneous surprise attacks from Silesia and East Prussia and so destroy the bulk of the Polish army west of the Vistula before the Poles had time to mobilize. By 20 August all preparations had to be completed. Commenting on the preliminary timetable submitted to him on 22 June, Hitler emphasized the crucial importance of the surprise element for securing the quick victory he had to have in the east. On his instructions the army build-up was again disguised as autumn manœuvres. And he refused to permit the evacuation of hospitals near the frontier (for casualty reception) to begin in July as army command proposed. The next day the defence council discussed preparations for the mobilization of labour for essential war work and also the problem of transportation. Whatever deep game Hitler may have been playing, the record of these deliberations, presided over by Goering, leaves one in no doubt that civilian ministers and army commanders believed war inevitable.

The diplomacy of the Great Powers in the summer of 1939 can only have encouraged Hitler to believe that he could isolate Poland. Initial alarm in London and Paris after the entry into Prague was soon replaced by growing reluctance to support Poland. The exchange of views with Moscow which commenced in April were conducted with noticeable restraint and completely without enthusiasm on the British side. Only late in July did Britain and France agree to staff talks in Moscow. Meanwhile Goebbels exploited the lacunae in Poland's position with merciless accuracy; the return of a German city to the *Reich* was scarcely a reason for the west to go to war; and even if the Poles were obstinate enough to fight, could they rely on allies who had betrayed the Czechs?

By the end of the summer all the evidence suggested that a confrontation with Poland was unavoidable. One last-minute arrangement made the attack absolutely certain: the Non-Aggression Pact with Russia. This notorious agreement between the Nazis and the Communists took the west completely by surprise. Although the western powers had never been really anxious to conclude an alliance with Russia, they never supposed in their wildest moments that a Nazi–Soviet Pact was a practical possibility in view of Hitler's long-standing aversion to bolshevism. The factor they overlooked was Hitler's utter lack of scruple and his skill as a power politician.

Oddly enough, other Nazi *Realpolitiker* were much more anxious than the Führer to approach Russia. Early in 1939 Goering was pressing for a new trade agreement with Russia to secure badly-needed raw materials. By mid-March negotiations were reluctantly suspended by the Germans since their badly-stretched economy could not guarantee prompt deliveries of the capital goods Russia required. In mid-April Goering was already toying with the idea of a political agreement, a proposal likely to meet with approval in the foreign office with its pro-Russian traditions and in army circles where Poland had never been popular.

When Russia took the initiative in seeking better relations with Germany, Hitler still hesitated. Towards the end of May another practitioner of the art of power politics, Ribbentrop, ordered the German ambassador, Schulenberg, to seek an agreement with Russia. Hitler, conscious of the enormity of the *volte-face* in the making and fearful of a Russian rebuff, cancelled the instructions on 25 May, only to order them to be dispatched, after all, on 30 May. Possibly not until the end of July did Hitler finally decide on a *rapprochement* with Russia at all costs. For only then did the foreign office introduce a note of desperate urgency into their instructions to Schulenburg. Simultaneously, the German propaganda campaign against Poland, which had lost its impetus in July, was revitalized and enlarged to include German claims to Posen and Upper Silesia.

A few days later the most serious crisis to date in the Danzig affair occurred. The Danzig Nazis informed the Polish customs officials on 4 August they they would no longer be allowed to perform their duties. The Polish government demanded immediate withdrawal of the order. Whereupon the Danzig Nazis denied its existence. On 9 August Germany warned Poland that a repetition of the 'ultimatum' would gravely imperil relations between them. To which Poland coolly retorted that she would resist attempts to infringe her legal rights in Danzig and regarded German intervention as aggression.

The irresistible force had at last encountered the immovable object. When Carl Burckhardt, League of Nations high commissioner in Danzig, visited Hitler on 11 August the latter was beside himself with rage.[9] 'If the slightest incident happens now,' he screamed, 'I shall crush the Poles without warning in such a way that no trace of Poland can be found afterwards. I shall strike like lightning with the full force of a mechanized army.' Warned by Burckhardt that this meant general war, Hitler retorted 'better today than tomorrow'. But, as so often on these occasions, he was still sufficiently in control of himself to make it clear that he did not seek war with the west. 'A free hand in the east was indispensable. If Germany had that he would gladly conclude a pact and guarantee British possessions,' he said, reverting fleetingly to his old dream of an Anglo-German understanding.

[9] C. Burckhardt, *Meine Danziger Mission, 1937–1939* (München, 1960), p. 348.

These remarks were undoubtedly intended for onward trans-
mission to London and were duly reported by Burckhardt.
More intriguing is the prophecy about Russia: 'Everything that I
have in mind is directed against Russia; if the west is too stupid
and too blind to grasp this then I will be forced to come to terms
with the Russians, to smash the west and after its defeat to turn
against Russia with all my forces. I need the Ukraine so that we
can't be starved out as in the last war.' Too much importance
should not be attached to one random passage. Nevertheless, it is
tempting to think that, in his anxiety to warn off the west, he
revealed for one fleeting moment the depth of his anti-bolshevism
implying that a Russian pact would be nothing more than an act
of pure power politics.[10]

As Germany's military preparations moved to a climax and the
prospect of agreement with Russia loomed on the horizon, Hitler's
determination to crush Poland hardened. Ribbentrop's eager
prompting played a part in this for his influence was at its zenith
in mid-August. When Ciano, sent to Germany by a worried
Mussolini anxious to know what his allies were planning, saw
Hitler on 12 August his worst fears were confirmed. Surrounded
by maps and deep in military calculations, Hitler informed Ciano
that Poland's speedy liquidation was essential in view of the
impending conflict with the west. In any case, 'it was unbearable
for a great power to have to tolerate perpetually such a hostile
neighbour only 150 kilometres from her capital.'[11] Therefore he
would utilize the next act of provocation to attack Poland at
once. Carried away by his own exuberance, he spoke of a life-
and-death struggle with the west following the defeat of Poland.
That would come later, he hastily informed his alarmed guest for
he was confident that the west would not fight over Poland. The
next day he admitted that there were deeper reasons for war than
irritation with Poland and the desire to eliminate a potential
enemy. Reverting to the theme of 23 May, he declared that 'the
German people requires to ensure for itself the materials which
are the guarantee of its existence. The operation against Poland
demonstrates the true road along which the German people
must march.'[12] Questioned about the timing of the attack, Hitler

[10] Oddly enough, Burckhardt suppressed these comments when reporting the
conversation.
[11] *DGFP*, D, VII, no. 43, p. 48.   [12] *Ciano's Diplomatic Papers*, p. 303.

revealed the extent to which military factors were making the
running in Germany (as they had done in July 1914). The army
estimated that it would take four to six weeks to subjugate
Poland. As mud and mist rendered roads and aerodromes un-
usable after 15 October, the attack must be launched by the end
of August. In other words, Poland had to be forced to declare her
hand to fit in with the military plans.

A prisoner of this tight military schedule, Hitler was now
obliged to speed up the Russian negotiations. On 14 August
Schulenburg asked Molotov to receive Ribbentrop in Moscow as
a matter of urgency. Casting all inhibitions aside, Ribbentrop
declared with brutal frankness that all territorial questions, the
Baltic, Poland and South-eastern Europe, could be settled to their
mutual satisfaction. The cautious Molotov agreed to receive him
but not until 26/27 August. Hitler intervened personally in the
negotiations and sent a telegram to Stalin asking him to receive
the foreign minister on 22/23 August in view of the mounting
tension with Poland. After twenty-four hours agonizing suspense
news arrived that Stalin had given way. Early on 22 August
Ribbentrop departed for Moscow.

The same day Hitler addressed a special conference of senior
commanders and their chiefs of staff at the Berghof.[13] Initially, so
he told them, he had favoured an understanding with Poland in
order to fight the west in a few years before turning eastwards –
an interesting admission giving some credence to the belief that
he was in some doubt about his next move after Munich. Once he
realized that Poland would attack Germany in the event of war in
the west, he resolved to deal with her first. The chances of western
intervention were slight. Britain was preoccupied with Far
Eastern and Mediterranean problems while French armaments
were outdated. But 'all these favourable circumstances will no
longer prevail in two or three years' time. No one knows how
much longer I shall have. Therefore better conflict now.'

With engaging frankness he admitted that Greater Germany
had been created by political bluff. But to use armies only as

[13] There are several versions; the most reliable by Admiral Boehm: *IMT*,
XVIII, Raeder–27. Also *DGFP*, D, VII, nos. 192–3; Halder's diary *DGFP*, D,
VII, appendix I. Cf. important article by W. Baumgart, 'Zur Ansprache Hitlers
vor den Führern der Wehrmacht am 22 August 1939', *VFZ*, 16, 1968; also Boehm
letter *VFZ*, 19, 1971.

instruments of bluff was extremely dangerous. The time had come to test the machine. Later on he spoke openly of his conviction that a long period of peace was positively harmful. 'Anyone who has thought seriously about the natural order knows that its meaning lies in the success of the best elements by means of force,' he remarked in terms reminiscent of *Mein Kampf*. Therefore in the struggle for living space his soldiers had to be 'harsh and remorseless' and 'steeled against all signs of compassion'.

There are some indications in this speech that Hitler was at last beginning to doubt whether Britain and France would after all surrender tamely over Poland. Not that he feared a long struggle at this stage. Probably the very most he expected was a purely token declaration of war to save face.[14] For, as he explained to the generals, how could the west aid Poland in practice? A British blockade would not hurt a Germany protected by autarky at home and able to draw on sources of supply in the east. An attack from the Maginot line was impossible and a western invasion of Belgium and Holland unlikely. The only hope of the 'little worms' in the west would have been a Russian alliance. Yet why should Russia bleed to death to please Britain? In fact, he declared triumphantly, Ribbentrop was already on his way to Moscow to sign a non-aggression pact on 24 August. This was not only the end of Poland. It also meant that Russia would supply grain, cattle, coal, lead and zinc to beat any blockade imposed by the west. This dramatic news undoubtedly impressed his audience. Some generals, such as Keitel, Brauchitsch and Manstein may have thought that Poland would capitulate without fighting. Most came away from the conference convinced that Poland would now be defeated without fear of western intervention, even nominal.[15]

Hitler seldom referred directly to the internal economic situation on these occasions. 22 August was an exception. Speaking of his reasons for going to war he remarked: 'It is easy for us to make decisions. We have nothing to lose; we have everything to gain. Because of our restrictions our economic situation is such

[14] Cf. Halder's diary p. 565: 'Führer would not take it amiss if England were to wage a sham war.'

[15] On the other hand army command believed that the west would intervene: E. Wagner, *Der Generalquartiermeister, Briefe und Tagebuchaufzeichnungen* (München –Wien, 1963), pp. 93–4.

that we can only hold out for a few more years. Goering can confirm this. We have no other choice; we must act.'

Economic difficulties undoubtedly became more acute in the first half of 1939. The gigantic arms increases ordered by Hitler in October 1938 could not be implemented in full; increased expenditure on arms simply added to inflationary pressures in the grossly-overloaded economy. In addition, Germany faced an acute steel shortage. She was producing only 1·85 million tons monthly at the end of 1938 to meet orders totalling 3·2 million tons. Faulty planning was one reason for the chaotic position. Equally to blame was the reluctance of Nazi leaders to face up to economic reality. Their stubborn refusal to curb expenditure on lavish building programmes or to curb consumer goods production can only have been due to a conviction that bread and circuses were essential for preserving dictatorial government in a country where despite *Gestapo* and concentration camp, discontent was never far below the surface. As long as overheating continued, labour shortages grew more pronounced and bottlenecks were unavoidable. Thus coal shortages occurred, not because output was inadequate, but because of transport shortages due to pressure on steel supplies. When the defence council met in June it was reported that transport inadequacies completely ruled out sudden mobilization and made a gradual concentration of forces against Poland, such as Hitler favoured for other reasons, absolutely mandatory.

Another problem facing Germany was the deteriorating financial situation. The situation became so acute that Keitel was obliged to cut military expenditure by one-third for the first half of 1939 owing to a shortage of liquid assets. The basic cause was the continuing refusal of the Nazis to cut government expenditure. Increased taxation and public loans failed to bridge the mounting deficit. To finance the ever-growing arms burden the *Reichsbank* borrowed short term. The result was an alarming increase of 3,000 million *RM* in note circulation between March and December 1938 compared with an increase of 1,700 millions over the preceding five years. To make matters worse, industrial profits fell due to higher taxation and rising prices which could not be passed on to consumers in their entirety. To maintain liquidity, businessmen discounted their *Mefo* bills which helped to increase note circulation when the economy was already

stretched beyond capacity. At last Schacht realized that Hitler
had no intention of checking inflation by repaying *Mefo* bills due in
the spring of 1939. Screwing up his courage, Schacht refused the
government new credits at the end of 1938 forcing the finance
minister to turn to private banks. On 2 January 1939 an irate
Hitler upbraided Schacht and denounced as 'mutiny' a *Reichsbank*
memorandum pleading for expenditure cuts. Shortly afterwards
Schacht and his colleagues were dismissed, the *Reichsbank*'s
independence ended, and it was soon apparent that the new
president, Funk, was nothing more than Hitler's chief cashier.
Hitler justified these steps to the Reichstag on 30 January by
arguing that economic policy depended not on 'financial theories'
but simply on the volume of production. More important, in the
last resort the country's future depended on the security of the
Reich abroad and therefore armaments must have the highest
priority. Needless to say, adding to existing debt was no answer to
the overheating problem – nor did it even produce the additional
arms Hitler wanted – and consequently the disturbing features
described elsewhere persisted.

How well prepared for war were the armed forces in September
1939? In the autumn the army reached its maximum peacetime
strength of fifty-two divisions. At the time of the Czech crisis there
were forty-eight divisions: thirty-nine infantry (including four
motorized), four armoured, one light, three mountain and one
cavalry. General mobilization would have produced only eight
reserve divisions and twenty-one *Landwehr* (third class) divisions
to make a grand total of seventy-seven divisions. Twelve months
later four new divisions had been created: one armoured and
three motorized. The position of reserves had improved dramatically because the effects of two-year compulsory service were
beginning to tell. By 1939 Germany had fifty reserve divisions so
that total mobilized strength was now 103 divisions, twenty-six
more than in 1938. Of these, seventy were fit for active service
and the remainder for static defence, By 1942 it was estimated
that Germany would have sufficient reserves to raise 150 divisions,
the maximum permitted by her arms-producing capacity. Therefore, Germany in 1939 could deal easily with Poland. Fifty-eight
divisions were concentrated on the Polish frontier, fifty-two of
these being regular divisions including all the armoured and
motorized units. The remaining ten regular divisions were ordered

to guard the West Wall supported by thirty-five divisions of third and fourth class reservists.

On the eve of war morale among senior officers was much higher than in 1938. There was much truth in Hitler's boast that he had 'fanatical 100% support' for the campaign.[16] In part this was because he had removed oppositional elements from the army after Munich but also because war with Poland was popular with the military and with the general public. Furthermore, unlike the situation in 1938, the generals were much more confident that the defences in the west, greatly strengthened in the past twelve months, could be held in the event of a French attack.

The airforce in 1939 enjoyed a measure of superiority *vis-à-vis* the airforces of potential opponents. It possessed about 3,000 machines including 1,180 medium bombers, 771 single-seater fighters and 336 dive bombers. The bulk of the aircraft consisted of Messerschmitt 108s (fighters) and Dornier 17s and Heinkel 111s (medium bombers), types produced in 1936 whereas British and French machines were of an earlier vintage. The danger for Germany was that once the western powers started to rearm in earnest, their airforces began to acquire machines of a slightly later design and better performance. Germany, it is true, was also beginning to re-equip with a new twin-engined fighter (Messerschmitt 110) and a new dive bomber (Junker 88) but had only small numbers of them in service in 1939. The hard fact was that from about mid-1939, as the British air attaché observed, the balance of air power was swinging against Germany; in short, if she was to benefit from her advantage, time had practically run out.[17] As the airforce was primarily a support weapon for the army – its aircraft had an operational radius of 500 kilometres – the absence of four-engined bombers for strategic bombing of cities and industrial installations did not matter; production of them had been stopped in 1937 to save aluminium. Only if a general war broke out would this weakness become serious, and even that could be offset by seizing bases in the Low Countries from which to attack Britain.

For the Polish campaign the navy's contribution was restricted to activity in the Baltic though the directive of 11 April did envisage the possibility of western intervention and instructed the

[16] *DGFP*, D, VI, no. 784.   [17] *DBFP*, III, iv, enclosure 117.

navy to deploy some forces in the North Sea. On 19 August Hitler ordered twenty-one submarines out to positions around the British Isles. A few days later two pocket battleships were sent into the Atlantic. These steps seem to confirm the hints in Hitler's speech on 22 August that he now accepted the distinct possibility of a British declaration of war though very probably only a nominal one.

On the economic front Germany's resources were adequate for war in the east. It is true that the Four Year Plan had not attained its targets. Germany was more dependent on foreign supplies of copper, lead and zinc than before 1933. The dependence of the steel industry on outside sources of supply was also considerable; even in 1941/2 Germany imported three times the amount of iron ore produced at home. All the same, much progress had been made since 1936. In 1939 Germany produced 22,000 tons of rubber sufficient to meet her military needs. And though difficulties arose in 1940, by 1942 rubber production exceeded demand. Aluminium output at 199,000 tons in 1939 was in excess of the target. In respect of oil it is true that early confidence in a solution of the problem inside eighteen months quickly evaporated. The target figure was revised downwards to 3·9 million tons for 1939. In fact Germany produced only 2·8 million tons annually of all types of fuel oil. But the significant statistic is that this figure represented four times the 1933 figure and twice the 1936 figure. In addition Germany had stocks of 492,000 tons of aircraft fuel, 991,000 tons of diesel oil and 451,000 tons of petrol. Furthermore, on the eve of the war important new commercial agreements improved the oil situation. In June Yugoslavia gave oil concessions to Germany and in July Roumania promised 400,000 tons of petroleum by January 1940 in exchange for German aircraft. Finally, in respect of food supplies, Germany was practically self-sufficient in bread, potatoes, sugar, milk and meat though still deficient in oils and fats of which 40 per cent were still imported. Bearing in mind Hitler's intention of waging *Blitzkrieg* warfare and of plundering occupied territory to recoup material losses, it can be said that Germany possessed adequate resources to make a bid for hegemony in Europe possible in 1939.

On 22 August Hitler informed his generals that the order for attack would be given later, probably on 26 August. The missing piece for which he waited impatiently at the Berghof was word from Moscow. On the evening of 23 August, after receiving news that the negotiations were going well, Hitler issued a provisional order for attack on 26 August, the final order to be given on 25 August. The pact with Russia was signed in the early hours of 24 August and Ribbentrop immediately departed for Berlin where Hitler awaited his arrival. The Führer's elation is recalled by Speer who recounts how Hitler, on receiving news of the agreement, banged the table, going red in the face as he shouted: 'I've got it, I've got it.'[18]

Not unnaturally he assumed that the western powers would be so stunned by the pact that they would lose all heart for war. Doubts began to assail him once again on 24 August when Chamberlain reaffirmed the Polish guarantee. In a clumsy attempt to neutralize Britain, Hitler immediately offered to guarantee the British Empire after first dealing with Poland. At the same time Hitler wrote to Mussolini explaining why he had not informed the Duce of negotiations with Russia and warning him that the attack on Poland was imminent. At 3 p.m. on 25 August Hitler issued the final order for attack to take place in the early hours of 26 August.

Two pieces of bad news upset Hitler's timetable. An hour after the final order was issued, news arrived in Berlin of the ratification of the Anglo-Polish treaty. Then at 6 p.m. Attolico informed Hitler that Italy could not go to war unless she was given large quantities of raw materials. A badly-shaken Führer at once stopped all troop movements and cancelled the attack: 'I need time for negotiations', he told Keitel.[19] It has been suggested that Hitler lost his nerve on 25 August and wavered for several days before recovering his composure on 30 August.[20] More likely, as Goering observed at Nuremberg, Hitler thought he might still be able to prevent British intervention by diplomatic manœuvres calculated to force Poland into an untenable position.[21] Dahlerus, Goering's Swedish friend, was sent to London to inform the government that Germany was ready to negotiate with Poland. However, when Henderson returned on 29 August with a

[18] A. Speer, *op. cit.*, p. 176.
[19] *IMT*, X, p. 514. Less dramatic than it sounds, for camouflaged mobilization continued and the next day, 26 August, he fixed the attack for 1 September subject to confirmation.
[20] L. Hill, *art. cit.*, p. 144.
[21] *NCA*, VIII, TC-90; cf. Halder's diary p. 565; O. Meissner, *op. cit.*, p. 518.

guarded reply, Hitler revealed more of his hand. Repeating the Godesberg technique, he raised his demands; Danzig and the Corridor must be returned to Germany and a Polish plenipotentiary must be sent to Berlin by 30 August; meanwhile Germany would prepare detailed proposals. It occurred to Henderson that Hitler planned to bully the Polish emissary into submision. What he did not fully realize was that if the Poles refused to comply with the ultimatum, the onus for war could be shifted onto their shoulders. Finally, in an interview with Ribbentrop at midnight on 30 August, Henderson proposed that normal diplomatic channels be used for negotiations instead of the summit diplomacy Hitler preferred. When Henderson went on to inquire what detailed proposals Germany had in mind, Ribbentrop angrily retorted that they now served no purpose in the absence of a Polish plenipotentiary, then gabbled through them at high speed and refused Henderson a copy. Nothing shows more clearly that Hitler had lost interest in the 'peace manœuvre'. For one thing, the diplomatic results had been disappointing. Furthermore, pressure from the military was growing. On 29 August Hitler told Henderson that the soldiers were impatient; a week had been lost and they could not afford another delay with the rainy season approaching. Therefore at 12.30 p.m. on 31 August Hitler gave the order for war. The sixteen points which Ribbentrop had refused to hand over were put to good propaganda use being broadcast on German radio at 9 p.m. The proposals, which provided for a plebiscite in the Corridor, guarantees of minority rights and the return of Danzig, created an impression of reasonableness quite belied by Hitler's determination to have his way with Poland. To justify the attack an incident was carefully staged at Gleiwitz.

At 4.45 a.m. on 1 September the cruiser *Schleswig-Holstein*, lying in Danzig harbour, opened fire on the Polish Westerplatte. Shortly afterwards German artillery opened fire along the Polish–German frontier and the Second World War commenced.

In some ways this is an unsatisfactory point at which to end the story. For it is, of course, only with hindsight that we regard the attack on Poland and the British and French declarations of war as the beginning of the end for Hitler. In fact, the *Blitzkrieg* stood him in good stead, first in Poland, then in Scandinavia, France, Belgium, Holland, Greece and Yugoslavia. Nor did Hitler accept that Britain had committed her all to a life-and-death struggle just because of her declaration on war on 3 September 1939. That was a temporary disappointment for him, nothing more. During the Dunkirk evacuation in 1940 he expressed the hope that Britain would now make peace so that he could have his hands free for 'his great and proper task: the confrontation with bolshevism'.[22] In fact the attack on Russia in 1941 was intended not only to establish German hegemony in Europe, but also to prove to Britain that it was useless to continue the struggle. For Hitler was reluctant to conclude that he was now engaged in that struggle for world hegemony with Britain which he had only intended to embark upon when he was undisputed master of Europe.

Reality broke in at last with the failure of the *Blitzkrieg* in Russia. Germany was now trapped into a long war in the east while Britain with American assistance prepared for a decisive onslaught in the west. Without complete control of the area from the Atlantic to the Urals Hitler could not possibly win. At the end of 1941 the first defensive orders were issued to units on the Russian front, and Hitler began at last to doubt whether his ambitions could be realized, though characteristically, he fought on with fanatical willpower for another three years trying to achieve the impossible.

[22] Quoted in A. Hillgruber, *op. cit.*, p. 145.

Bibliographical Note

Primary material of the highest importance is contained in *The Trial of the Major War Criminals before the International Military Tribunal* (Nuremberg, 1947–9), 42 vols. and *Nazi Conspiracy and Aggression* (Washington, 1946–8), 10 vols. Also indispensable are *Documents on British Foreign Policy, 1919–39, Documents on German Foreign Policy, 1918–1945* and *Documents diplomatiques français, 1932–1939.*

On Hitler *Mein Kampf* (various editions) and *Hitler's Secret Book* (New York, 1961) are essential sources. No definitive edition of his speeches exists but the most useful collections are N. Baynes, *The speeches of Adolf Hitler, 1922–1939* (OUP, 1942) and M. Domarus, *Hitler: Reden und Proklamationen, 1932–1945* (Münster, 1962–3). Hitler's rambling reminiscences in *Hitler's Table Talk, 1941–1944* (London, 1953) are occasionally illuminating; the German original edited by P. Schramm, *Hitlers Tischgespräche im Führerhauptquartier, 1941–42* (Stuttgart, 1963) is to be preferred. Though its authenticity has been questioned, much of H. Rauschning, *Hitler Speaks* (London, 1939) has the ring of truth about it. A. Bullock, *Hitler. A study in tyranny* (London, 1952) is still the best biography; the latest biographer W. Maser, *Adolf Hitler. Legende, Mythos Wirklichkeit* (München, 1971), adds new material on the early years. Bullock's picture of Hitler as the supreme opportunist is corrected by E. Jäckel, *Hitlers Weltanschauung. Entwurf einer Herrschaft* (Tübingen, 1969), an important re-appraisal of Hitler's ideology; Bullock now inclines to this view in 'Hitler and the origins of the Second World War' in *British Academy Proceedings*, LIII, 1967.

Among the vast army of memoirs, all of which cast some light on Hitler without resolving the riddle, the following cannot be ignored: A. François-Poncet, *The Fateful Years* (London, 1949); N. Henderson, *Failure of a Mission, 1937–39* (London, 1940); F. Hossbach, *Zwischen Wehrmacht und Hitler, 1934–1938* (Hanover, 1949); E. Kordt, *Wahn und Wirklichkeit. Die Aussenpolitik des Dritten Reiches* (Stuttgart, 1948) and *Nicht aus den Akten. Die Wilhelmstrasse in Frieden und Krieg* (Stuttgart, 1950); O. Meissner, *Staatssekretär unter Ebert-Hindenburg-Hitler* (Mannheim, 1950); F. von Papen, *Memoirs* (London, 1952); P. Schmidt, *Statist auf diplomatischer Bühne, 1932–1945* (Frankfurt, 1949); A. Speer, *Erinnerungen* (Frankfurt a.M./Berlin, 1969); E. von Weizsäcker, *Memoirs*

(Chicago, 1951); A. Zoller, *Hitler privat. Erlebnisbericht seiner Geheimsekretärin* (Düsseldorf, 1949). Some important material in *Ciano's Diaries, 1937–1938* (London, 1952); *Ciano's Diary, 1939–1943* (London, 1947) and *Ciano's Diplomatic* Papers (London, 1948).

Much work has been done on foreign policy especially on the immediate pre-war period. Quite outstanding is G. Weinberg, *The Foreign Policy of Hitler's Germany. Diplomatic Revolution in Europe, 1933–1936* (Chicago and London, 1970). There is nothing comparable for 1936–9. J. A. Jacobsen in his exhaustive study of party organizations *Nationalsozialistische Aussenpolitik* (Frankfurt, 1969) seems to show that they exerted little influence. K. Hildebrand, *Vom Reich zum Weltreich; Hitler, NSDAP und koloniale Frage, 1919–45* is important for colonial aspects. Useful on the foreign office is P. Seabury, *The Wilhelmstrasse. A study of German diplomats under the Nazi regime* (Univ. of California, 1955). The evolution of Hitler's policy before 1933 is studied in G. Schubert, *Anfänge nationalsozialistischer Aussenpolitik* (Köln, 1963). On Austria the best works are J. Gehl, *Austria, Germany and the Anschluss, 1931–39* (London, 1963) and D. Roos, *Hitler und Dollfuss. Die deutsche Österreichpolitik, 1933–34* (Hamburg, 1966). On Poland D. Roos, *Polen und Europa. Studien zur Aussenpolitik, 1931–39* (Tübingen, 1957). M. Funke examines German policy during the Abyssinian crisis in *Sanktionen und Kanonen, Hitler Mussolini und der nationale Abessinienkonflikt, 1934–1936* (Düsseldorf, 1970). On the Czech crisis see especially B. Celovsky. *Das Münchener Abkommen von 1938* (Stuttgart, 1958) and on the role of Slovakia in Hitler's strategy J. K. Hoensch, *Die Slowakei und Hitlers Ostpolitik* (Köln, 1965).

The serious study of Nazi economic policy is getting under way at long last. On the relationship between rearmament and economic policy B. Carroll, *Total War. Arms and economics in the Third Reich* (Hague/Paris, 1968) is excellent; as is Chapter I of A. S. Milward, *The German Economy at War* (London, 1965). There is much useful material in B. H. Klein, *Germany's Economic Preparations for War* (Harvard, 1959) though he greatly underestimates Germany's commitment to war in 1939. R. Erbe, *Die nationalsozialistische Wirtschaftspolitik, 1933–39 im Licht der modernen Theorie* (Zürich, 1958) is a first-rate study but strictly economic. There is no definitive biography of Schacht. Both E. N. Peterson, *Hjalmar Schacht. For and against Hitler. A politico-economic study of Germany, 1923–1945* (Boston, 1954) and A. E. Simpson, *Hjalmar Schacht in Perspective* (Hague/Paris, 1969) are favourably disposed; for a trenchant criticism consult K. D. Bracher, W. Sauer, G. Schultz, *Die nationalsozialistische Machtergreifung* (Köln Opladen, 1960). The only work on the Four Year Plan is D. Petzina, *Autarkie im Dritten Reich. Der nationalsozialistische Vierjahresplan* (Stuttgart, 1968). On synthetic fuel W. Birkenfeld, *Der synthetische Treibstoff, 1939–1945. Ein Beitrag zur nationalsozialistischen Wirtschaft und Rüstungspolitik* (Göttingen, 1964). On steel J. J. Jäger, *Die wirtschaftliche*

Abhängigkeit des Dritten Reiches vom Ausland dargestellt am Beispiel der Stahl-industrie (Köln, 1969). A. Schweitzer, *Big Business in the Third Reich* (London, 1964) does not quite live up to expectations. Important articles by T. W. Mason: 'Some origins of the Second World War' (a critique of A. J. P. Taylor's book of that name) and 'Labour in the Third Reich, 1933–39' in *Past and Present* for 1964 and 1966 respectively. The work of East German historians should not be neglected. Important material on I.G. Farben in D. Eichholtz, *Geschichte der deutschen Kriegswirtschaft, 1939–1945* (Berlin, 1969) vol. I; also D. Eichholtz and W. Schuman, *Anatomie des Krieges Neue Dokumente über die Rolle des deutschen Monopolkapitals bei der Vorbereitung und Durchführung des zweiten Weltkrieges* (Berlin, 1969). Useful for the general Marxist standpoint is D. Eichholtz's review of the works of Birkenfeld, Petzina and Schweitzer in *Jahrbuch für Wirtschaftsgeschichte*, III, 1971.

On the military side historians have mostly concentrated on the army and on the generals' opposition to Hitler. For the present study R. O'Neill. *The German Army and the Nazi Party* (London, 1966) is indispensable, as is G. Meinck, *Hitler und die deutsche Aufrüstung, 1933–39* (Wiesbaden, 1959) though nothing after 1937. Fairly useful is E. M. Robertson, *Hitler's Pre-war Policy and Military Plans* (London, 1963). Statistical information in B. Müller-Hildebrand, *Das Heer, 1933–45* Bd. I *Das Heer bis zum Kriegsbeginn* (Stuttgart, 1969). J. Leuschner examines the relationship between foreign policy and military strategy with particular reference to 1938 in *Volk und Raum. Zum Stil der nationalsozialistischen Aussenpolitik* (Göttingen, 1961). Also important is W. Bernhardt, *Die deutsche Auf-rüstung, 1934–39. Militärische und politische Konzeptionen und ihre Eins-chätzung durch die Alliierten* (Frankfurt, 1969). On the navy F. Hinsley, *Hitler's Strategy* (Cambridge, 1951) rather outdated. There is an important article by R. Bensel, 'Die deutsche Flottenpolitik von 1933 bis 1939. Eine Studie über die Rolle des Flottenbaus in Hitlers Aussenpolitik' in *Marine Rundschau Beiheft 3*, 1958. Also C.-A. Gemzel, *Raeder, Hitler und Skandivavien. Der Kampf für einen maritimen Operationsplan* (Lund, 1965). The airforce has been somewhat neglected by historians. Finally, though dealing with a later period, the profound analysis of A. Hillgruber, *Hitlers Strategie Politik und Kriegsführung, 1940–1941* (Frankfurt a.M.) is of great value.

Indispensable periodicals for the study of this period are *Viertel-jahrshefte für Zeitgeschichte* (often containing valuable primary material) and the *Jahrbuch für Wirtschaftsgeschichte*.

Chronological Table

		Economic Development	Progress of Rearmament
		Foreign Policy	*Economic Development*	*Progress of Rearmament*

1933		Foreign Policy	Economic Development	Progress of Rearmament
	Jan.	Hitler appointed Chancellor	Six million unemployed	Army of 100,000; 10 divisions
	Feb.	Germany attends Disarmament Conference		
	March		Schacht appointed *Reichsbank* president	
	June		Reinhardt plan to reduce unemployment	
	Oct.	Germany leaves Disarmament Conference and League of Nations		
1934				
	Jan.	Non-Aggression Pact with Poland		Secret law reduces period of service from 12 to 1 year
	Feb.			Fritsch appointed C-in-C with orders to expand army
	June		Balance of payments difficulties Schacht appointed minister of economics	Expansion begins in earnest
	July	Dollfuss murdered		
	Sept.		Schacht's New Plan	
	Oct.			Army now 240,000; 24 divisions
1935				
	March	Re-introduction of conscription		Hitler orders expansion to 36 divisions
	June	Anglo-German Naval Convention		

		Foreign Policy	Economic Development	Progress of Rearmament
	Oct.		'Bread Crisis'	Plan Red drawn up
1936				
	March	Re-occupation of Rhineland	Fuel crisis	
	April		Goering takes charge of raw materials and foreign exchange	
	June	Austro-German agreement		
	July	Spanish Civil War begins	Financial crisis	
	Aug.		Hitler's Memorandum	Period of conscription extended to 2 years
	Sept.		Four Year Plan begins	
	Dec.		Full employment achieved	
1937				
	Spring			Plan Green drawn up
	Nov.	Rome–Berlin Axis; Hossbach meeting	Schacht resigns as minister of economics	
	Dec.			Plan Green takes precedence over red
1938				
	Jan.			Blomberg/Fritsch dismissals; Hitler assumes command of armed forces
	Feb.	Hitler–Schuschnigg meeting		
	March	Invasion of Austria		
	April			Hitler plans attack on Czechoslovakia
	June		Decrees on wage maxima and compulsory labour service	
	Aug.		Emergency plan for production of war material	

		Economic Development	Progress of Rearmament
	Foreign Policy		
Sept.	Czech crisis		Army now 550,000; 48 divisions plus 24 reserve divisions
Oct.			Hitler orders massive expansion of armed forces
1939			
Jan.		Schacht dismissed from *Reichsbank*	Hitler approves Z Plan for naval expansion
March	Destruction of Czechoslovakia		
March	British guarantee to Poland		
April	Hitler denounces non-aggression pact with Poland and Anglo-German convention		Hitler orders preparations for attack on Poland
May	Pact of Steel		
Aug.	Russo-German Non-Aggression Pact		
Sept.	Attack on Poland begins		Army now 52 divisions plus 50 reserve divisions

Index